# GOOD
# NEWS
## IN BAD TIMES

# GOOD
# NEWS
## IN BAD TIMES

DISCOVERING SPIRITUAL MEANING IN
THE MIDST OF CRISIS AND UNCERTAINTY

JOHN P. LOZANO

Kairos
Missions Press

# GOOD NEWS IN BAD TIMES

*Discovering Spiritual Meaning in the Midst of Crisis and Uncertainty*
*John P. Lozano*

Edited by Andrew Yankech
Cover Design, Book Design, and Typesetting by Michael Babin

Published by Kairos Missions Press

GOOD NEWS IN BAD TIMES is distributed by:
ACTA Publications, 4848 N. Clark Street, Chicago, IL 60640
(800) 397-2282, www.actapublications.com

Library of Congress Number: 2010924662
ISBN: 978-0-9844868-0-9
Printed in The United States by Versa Press on 30% PCW recycled paper
Year 16 15 14 13 12 11 10
Printing 05 04 03 02 First Edition

# CONTENTS

## To Helen

*For the love that bears all things, believes all things,*
*hopes all things, endures all things.*

# INTRODUCTION

In the prologue to his book *The Gates of the Forest,*
Elie Weisel retells this Hasidic tale:

> *When the great Rabbi Israel Baal Shem-Tov saw*
> *misfortune threatening the Jews, it was his custom to*
> *go into a certain part of the forest to meditate. There*
> *he would light a special fire and say a secret prayer.*
> *Then a miracle would happen and the misfortune*
> *would be averted. Years later when his disciple, the*
> *celebrated Magid of Mezritch, needed to intercede with*
> *heaven, he went to the same place in the forest and*
> *said: "Master of the Universe, listen! I do not know how*
> *to light the fire, but I am still able to say the prayer."*

*And again a miracle would happen and disaster would be averted. Still later, Rabbi Moshe-Lieb of Sasov, in order to save his people once more, went into the forest and said: "I do not know how to light the fire, I do not know the prayer, but I know the place and this must be sufficient." It was, and the miracle occurred.*

*Then it fell to Rabbi Israel of Rizhyn to overcome misfortune. Sitting in his armchair, his head in his hands, he spoke to God: "I am unable to light the fire and I do not know the prayer. I cannot even find the place in the forest. All I can do is to tell the story, and this must be sufficient." And it was.*

God created humanity because God loves stories.

We all have a story to tell. Human history, and the Bible itself, is a series of stories. If we listen carefully, we can often find ourselves in the stories we hear. We discover how connected we are, for we are all linked together by one thing—our humanity. In this common humanity and life we share, we have all experienced something profoundly good and profoundly unsettling along the way. Our stories often involve struggle and it is precisely in the struggle, the misfortune, that we move towards God, to the consideration of something greater than ourselves. This journey is not easy and often our words are inadequate to express this movement, but we all have our stories. As the story above shows, that is enough.

When I think of the stories of our lives, I am often reminded of Anne Frank, a young Jewish girl who lived in Nazi Germany. Even in the midst of the horrendous treatment she suffered, she was still able to write the following in her famous diary:

> *Everyone has inside him a piece of good news.*
> *The good news is that you don't know how great*
> *you can be! How much you can love! What you*
> *can accomplish! And what your potential is.*

While most of us will never come close to experiencing the kind of struggle Anne faced, we all can speak of turmoil and pain in our personal lives. The daily struggles of living in our modern and harried times, the stress of job loss or financial ruin, a life-threatening illness—these are the struggles and misfortunes that we face. How we respond to them is what defines us. What if Anne is right, that we all have a piece of good news within us, a potential to love that is present even in the midst of great sadness or misfortune? That might change how we understand the struggles we face, how we view our stories and our potential to discover happiness and spiritual meaning in this life—even in the midst of confusion, struggle, and pain.

In the following pages you will read true stories of people who have discovered and responded to a special invitation, an invitation for "more." This invitation has brought with it the potential for greater happiness, a deeper understanding of life, and a call to spiritual awakening. I believe these stories are about all of us and for all of us, for each one testifies to our common human intuition about life and the possibilities before us. While our shared humanity is our pure gift and glory, it is also our grief and anguish. But like Anne Frank said, our humanity holds an abundance of "good news." The good news is that our humanity speaks, and if we listen to our collective human experience, we will hear it call out to us, invite us, even lure us into considering that there is more to this life, to who we are, and to the reality of God for each of us.

In the second part of this book, we will examine another story, that of Jesus of Nazareth and how some people have come to understand the ways in which the gospel message speaks to our human experience and opens up radically new possibilities for life and spiritual growth.

In short, this book is a practical strategy for a new way to examine and respond to the predictable and the unpredictable elements in life. This book offers a new way to respond to our successes as well as our failures, to find new opportunity for our lives, our faith, and ways of being in this world. It offers a path for each of us to discover, especially in difficult times, a new spiritual way of seeing and understanding, a kind of spiritual "right-sizing" if you will—putting things in their proper perspective and place in our life. This book is for all of us who have ever wondered, "Is there more to life than this?"

The good news is...there is!

# PART I

# LISTENING

I AM COMPULSIVE ABOUT ONE THING, at least one I will admit to publicly: directions. When I go on a trip, I really like to know where I am going and the best way to get there. I make a point to check maps, call ahead to my destination for directions, go to MapQuest.com for detailed driving instructions, and make whatever preparations are necessary before I set out. Naturally, when I heard about the invention of GPS navigation systems, I thought that investing in one would be a dream come true.

For someone like me, this system is great. It tells me how to get where I want to go, and does so in several different ways. I can choose to follow text or an image, and the GPS device will tell me the quickest and the cheapest way to get to where I'm going. If I encounter bad traffic or an accident, it will give me alternative routes.

Best of all, it will *speak* to me—and I can even pick out its voice. If I wanted to, I could make my GPS sound like Mr. T (though I don't know why anyone would want to hear his voice saying, "Go left, you fool!"). When I bought my GPS, I decided instead that I would opt for a sweet female voice with a lovely British accent.

Shortly after I had purchased this new system, my friend Jim and I planned a hiking trip to the Pocono Mountains. Since we were coming from different locations, we decided to meet at an exit off the Pennsylvania Turnpike, leave one of our cars, and drive the rest of the way together. Jim said, "Let's meet at the Quakertown exit." I agreed, thinking to myself, *I know where that is, it's on the turnpike west. I've driven by it many times.*

(It is actually on the northeast extension of the turnpike.)

Even though I assumed I knew where I was going, I thought I would take my GPS along just for fun to see how well it worked and to get accustomed to it. It was only a few minutes into my trip when that sweet female voice with the lovely British accent began to say, "Wrong way, turn around. Wrong way, turn around."

My first thought was, *I can't believe it. She is wrong.* Then I thought, *I must be taking an alternative route, not the one she would choose. Eventually she will catch up with me, and she will re-route herself to my way of going.*

That did not happen.

"Wrong way, turn around. Wrong way, turn around. Wrong way, turn around."

Ten minutes, twenty minutes, thirty minutes....

"Wrong way, turn around."

By this time her voice was no longer sweet. Forty minutes later, I finally stopped my car and called my friend, only to discover that I was indeed going in the wrong direction. Once I had turned around and started heading for the Quakertown exit (did I mention it was forty minutes in the opposite direction?), I had a moment of insight into myself....

*Why is it that I assume I am going the right way?*

A scary thought crossed my mind: How often do I assume I am going the right way when in reality I am not...and I do not know it?

I assume that my current thinking is correct, purely because it is my way of thinking, when I am far more wrong than I could imagine.

And why am I wrong?

Because I am not listening.

One of the most important skills we can develop in life is the ability to listen. Most human conflict is a breakdown of communication, and this breakdown often occurs when we do not hear or fully understand what the other person means by their words or actions. We assume that our interpretation of what he or she is saying is correct, but often it is not. Letting this miscommunication continue over time creates a false understanding of the other person and a bias that becomes a lens through which we see them. Once this lens becomes hardened, we see everything the other person does and says through that lens.

How often do we say or hear someone else say, "What I hear you saying is…. Am I correct?" Yet how much miscommunication and conflict could be avoided with that simple question, one that only requires a bit more *effort*? Effort plays a far bigger role in good communication than we are likely to admit. Along with effort, *humility* is a key component in healthy communication, though not a common word these days. It requires some humility not to assume that I am always right in my interpretations. Listening with effort and humility creates a bedrock of good communication upon which healthy relationships can be built.

If effort and humility are necessary in human relationships, they are even more necessary in the arena of religious faith and the discovery of spiritual meaning. Perhaps miscommunications in our past have also created misunderstandings in our spiritual formation. Or perhaps we assume we are correct in our understanding, even though we may not be. Like human relationships, this "miscommunication" may go on for some time only to eventually be formed into a bias through which we proceed to see all of religious belief and activity. Often I hear someone say, "Yeah, I have been to church, and my parents are Christian. I have heard it all before." I find myself thinking: *Really? All of it?*

Is there a new understanding possible in the area of faith and spirituality for us? If so, then I think it would come through the same two qualities required of good communication between human beings: effort and humility. When it comes to finding a new understanding about faith, effort is required to investigate with an open and patient mind and heart. Humility is required to truly listen to what the results of our investigations are saying and accept that our preconceived notions may be wrong.

This openness to new possibilities in our understanding of faith is what happened to me when I was driving back, in the right direction, to meet my friend. Along the way I had another insight. I began to think about how much technology and human intellectual power went into creating the GPS system. All the work and skill of brilliant people, all the huge, intricate, sophisticated satellites out there in space, all the millions of dollars invested into my GPS system—all of this that is directing me and this little car of mine. Even though I realize this, I still think that I am right. I even paid money for the thing! If I had allowed myself the humility to think that I might not quite know how to get to my destination, and if I had expended the effort to use the functions of my GPS device and view my route on a map, I might have avoided getting lost.

Humanity often makes similar assumptions when it comes to the mystery of God and faith. If you are like me, you may recognize how often we believe that we already know all there is to know about the world and how it operates, even in spite of growing evidence that maybe we do not. We go around thinking, in subtle ways, that we are so advanced in our knowledge but that Christianity is lagging behind, a bit outdated. There is a part of us, a deep place, where we really think that Christianity, even God, will catch up with us someday.

How much has already been given us in our quest for God! Billions of believers, Jew and Christian, have trusted that God speaks through this book we call the Bible, giving us guidance on where to go and how to live, revealing something of the very nature of God for over 3,000 years. Along with this, billions of people in faith communities have pondered and prayed and struggled to help themselves and others know something of the mystery of God and the ways God can be known.

All of this has already been given to us, given as a gift. We have been offered an incredible guidance system, and yet we still think we know better and refuse to listen. We close our ears to God's lovely, sweet, gentle voice—a voice that is soft, quiet, and almost imperceptible because God respects our freedom to choose to listen or not. God always gives us a choice. The voice of God's spirit wants to speak to us and reveal itself, reveal who we are and how to live, but it is always gentle and quiet.

Often we are we like the *Peanuts* character Charlie Brown. One day he was practicing archery in his backyard. Instead of aiming at the target, he chose to shoot an arrow at the fence and then walk over and draw a target around wherever the arrow struck. Lucy walked up and said, "Why are you doing that, Charlie Brown?"

He replied without embarrassment, "This way I never miss."

Could it be that we are like Charlie Brown in some fundamental way, not admitting the possibility that we are missing the mark? What if we could get to the place where we admit that maybe, just maybe, we are wrong, or that we do not know everything we need to know to live well, that the way we view the world, the way we use our time, our talents, and our money, the way we live our emotional lives, how we look at God, ourselves, and other people might just be a little off.

If we could get to this place of humility and openness, it would be good for us. Perhaps this is the disposition required so that something new might happen in our lives, so that our "just adequate" circumstances might change. In order to change where we are and arrive at a place where we know and understand that there is more to this life, we must begin with a humble attitude and sincere effort to listen so that we may discover the new life that we are being offered.

Often this comes about precisely during the experience of crisis, when we feel the earth beneath us shifting, when so much of what we once took for granted can no longer be counted on. Initially our reaction is one of confusion, worry, and imbalance. We can drink it away, deny it is happening, or we can "listen" to what it is saying to us. Where will I place my trust now? What is most important to me? Am I alone in all this? We may discover a new person to trust, something of new and greater importance, or that we are not alone and never have been. We would be in a good position to hear that sweet, soft, gentle voice of the one who loves us and always has.

In the book *Prince Caspian* by C. S. Lewis, the character Lucy, her older sister, and two brothers are on a quest to find Aslan (the lion who represents Christ in the story) at a time of great crisis and turmoil. At one point Lucy announces with heartfelt joy that she has seen Aslan. He is with them. It is so wonderful. Everything will work out in the end. Her older siblings initially ridicule her since they have not seen him. Later on, the older siblings finally see Aslan as well, and Lucy's older sister Susan turns and asks why she could not see Aslan earlier as Lucy did. Lucy answers, "Because you were not listening."

Listening is critical. There are new dimensions to discover that are reserved only for those who listen, and it begins with listening to life, to what is around us, to that which we have experienced up to this point in our lives.

. . .

## PERSONAL REFLECTION

*Think of a time when you were absolutely certain you were right about something or someone, only to later discover you were wrong. How did you feel? What did you learn from that experience and how has it shaped your behavior since then?*

# WE ARE
# WORTH MORE

*"There's gotta be more than this."*
*~ Tom Brady*

O NE SUNDAY EVENING WHILE WATCHING
television, I came across an interview on *60 Minutes* with
Tom Brady. The highly successful quarterback for the
New England Patriots was smiling broadly, as he often does, and
he seemed to be enjoying the interview as he spoke of his money,
fame, and career success. Then he suddenly became serious and
said, "Why do I have three Super Bowl rings and still think there
is something greater out there for me? Maybe a lot [of people]
would say, 'This is what it is' ... me, I think, 'God, there's gotta be
more than this.'"

Interviewer Steve Kroft asked, "What is the answer?"

Brady replied, "I wish I knew... I wish I knew."

I was stunned to hear Brady thinking aloud like this. Here is someone that really has "everything." He is young, good looking, and at the age of twenty-eight had already won three Super Bowl titles. He has more money, success, and fame than most anyone else alive today and at the time was dating some of the most beautiful women in the world. On top of this, Brady seems to be a really nice guy, a happy person with a great family of parents and siblings whom he loves and enjoys spending time with. So I was genuinely surprised to hear him say, in all seriousness, "There's gotta be more than this."

Tom Brady lives what many, if not most, people today consider to be "the good life." For him to wonder and question his own satisfaction is remarkable. But I think he speaks for us all. There is something within each of us that wonders, *Is this all there is?* Something within us answers with the word "no," and like Tom Brady, we often think to ourselves, *There is more, there has to be more.* We can understand how this question of "more" arises in times of difficulty, stress, uncertainty, and loss, but what is so remarkable is how it comes forth even in the midst of success. This nagging, relentless pondering points to the universal and deeply human nature of this question.

We are not the only ones who have thought like this. The great fourth-century philosopher and theologian Augustine of Hippo is a man who many scholars believe to be the first person in western history to write in a psychologically reflective way. Like Tom Brady, Augustine of Hippo was a man who "had it all." He was brilliant, well-connected in society, well-traveled, a resident of some of the greatest centers of culture and education. He was involved in the most fashionable and popular movements of his day, lived unmarried with a woman, and enjoyed all life had to offer. Yet even in the midst of this, Augustine writes of a restlessness within that gnawed at his mind and heart and would not leave him, a restlessness that drove his many pursuits.

Augustine is often quoted as saying, "You have made us for yourself, oh Lord, and our heart is restless until it rests in you." Why is this quote, of all of Augustine's incredibly prolific writings, the one most repeated by others throughout history? Perhaps it speaks of something we all know and experience within ourselves. We see this in the seventeenth-century French scientist and philosopher Blaise Pascal, who said something very similar: "We are made with a God-shaped hole that only God can fill."

I see this restlessness in my own life as well. I've had this experience, and perhaps you have too: I am looking out the window on a Sunday night, after all the weekend activities are finished, facing a new week ahead. There is a moment of quiet until suddenly a vacant place opens up inside the pit of my stomach. A feeling of emptiness, a frightening place, a hole. And in that space, something inside me asks, *Is this all there is? Is there nothing more? Am I alone?* Normally I would just turn on the television, listen to music, keep busy, push it away…but it comes back. It comes back out of nowhere, completely uninvited, and with it comes a pressing realization:

*There has to be more. There must be more. This cannot be all there is.*

From the perspective of faith, real life begins here. It begins in the experience of our humanity, an experience within of discomfort and disquiet that raises questions for us. However, this human experience may exist within us for a purpose: to point us to something new, to possibilities we have yet to consider. Considering new and unknown possibilities is not easy, so we spend little time listening to this discomfort. We ignore it and push it away, and we fear the possible result of it all ending in frustration and disappointment if we discover there is nothing more, and this realization may be too much to bear.

But there is another possibility, that of beginning something unknown, of understanding ourselves, our lives, and God in a new way that would lead to a better, fuller, richer life. This common human longing may be a sign to us that "something more" does, in fact, exist. Perhaps the restlessness itself exists as a way of saying, "Trust. You are wired this way for a reason." Let it take you somewhere, perhaps to a new place, a life, a new sense of who you are and what your life is all about, perhaps a life more wonderful than you have yet considered or even dreamed possible. As Anne Frank would say, our humanity holds an abundance of "good news"—the good news of what you can become, what you can accomplish, how much you can love.

Being open to this kind of change may not come easy for us, but it lies at the very heart of a new understanding of life and faith.

## WHY BOTHER?

Normally we run from the task of looking honestly at ourselves, and one of the main ways we do this is by focusing on ways to change other people instead of trying to improve ourselves. Whether consciously or unconsciously, we think, *If this person or these circumstances were different, my life would be better.* Or, *It is about them—they are the cause of my unrest, not me.* Or, perhaps these situations are slightly more familiar: a husband who struggles with anger and instead of changing how he deals with it decides to blame his wife for his actions. Conversely, a wife who is constantly anxious and short-tempered does not accept this nor address it as her own issue but decides instead to blame her children as the cause for her impatience. In truth, it's painfully clear that we all have tried at some point to change those around us—but it will always remain that the only people we can change are ourselves. Of all the lessons in life, this is perhaps the most difficult and most important one to learn, and if it not learned it undoubtedly leads to heartache.

If we take an honest look at ourselves, we should see many things we admire and other things we would very much like to change. Often we sense our own inability to change ourselves and feel "stuck" with the person we are. We end up throwing our hands in the air, saying, "This is just who I am, so why bother changing? I have tried over and over. Why not just leave well enough alone?"

Well, there are two reasons why we should not "leave well enough alone." First, things are not "well enough." Second, we are worth more.

A truthful and honest inventory of ourselves will reveal to us our inner conflicts, contradictions, emotional battles, hurts, fears, insecurities, and broken relationships with others—and all of these point to the glaring truth that things are not "well enough." We often feel powerless before these truths of ourselves and may flock to self-help books, conferences, diets, lectures, and the like, trying to gain some personal power. All of these things can be good and certainly worth pursuing to an extent. But then that moment comes when we know that not a single self-help book comes close to reaching us, to getting us "un-stuck," and we begin to sense something innate to our humanity which is keeping us stagnant, unfulfilled, and lackluster.

If there *is* more to this life, then we must, at the very least, consider pursuing it. If human development points to the possibility of changing for the better, then why would we not do all we can to see just how far we can go, how much is possible for us in this life? And that brings us to the second reason why none of us should leave well enough alone: *We are worth more.* To love and accept ourselves as worthy of happiness is profoundly important. If we do not love ourselves we will never expect love from others. We will always settle for less, never coming to believe that any significant, positive life change is possible.

Many years ago I was a high school teacher. There was a young woman in one of my classes who, by anyone's standards, was physically beautiful. She was also intelligent, well-spoken, and responsible—a fine person and a pleasure to have in class. One day she came in with a black eye. After class we spoke and she reported how her boyfriend had become very upset and hit her. After a while, he returned to her and apologized. I asked what happened next. She replied that she "slept with him again that night." It was a moment in which I did not know how to respond. I thought to myself, "Does she not see what I see, does she not see that she is worthy of so much more?"

We are all that young woman. We are all worthy of more. It is sad how often we do not believe this. Why else would we enter into behavior that clearly does not lead to happiness? How often I have heard someone say, "Well, I really didn't want to ___, but I felt I had to." To act in ways in which we are not true to ourselves, to settle for less, the status quo in which we find ourselves, is a very sad way to live.

What prevents us from recognizing our worth and thus settling for less than we deserve? Is it because we feel powerless to change, or is it because we don't think we are worth more than this? Are we settling for whatever reality we find ourselves in? Do we simply buy into what everyone around us is telling us—do we buy into this culture, this time in history simply because we find ourselves here? Is this all that really matters? Is it all there is?

Or could there be something more?

The more we ponder these questions, the more we come to realize that left to ourselves, the best we can hope for is an adequate life. Yet we know that "adequate" falls far short of the dreams we have for ourselves. We want more than "adequate" and we deserve more. It is imperative that we realize we cannot leave "well enough alone," that changing ourselves is of the utmost importance if it means living a life that is more than just "adequate." Once we accept that there could be more for us, then the only remaining question that each of us must ask ourselves is not whether or not I must change, but rather *how* I will change.

· · ·

## PERSONAL REFLECTION

*Have you ever experienced that sense within that there must be more? Perhaps you enjoyed a professional or financial success, but felt like something was missing. Did you explore that feeling. What did it say to you?*

# CHANGE

*"Courage is not simply one of the virtues*
*but the form of every virtue."*
~C. S. Lewis

Y OU'VE PROBABLY HEARD IT SAID BEFORE
that the only constant in life is change. But have you ever
stopped to consider what this really means? Change is
inevitable. It follows us throughout our lives whether we like it
or not. Our bodies change as we age: the texture of our skin, the
numbers on the scale, the amount of hair on our heads. Our jobs
change, our finances change, our relationships change, our opinions
change. Indeed, with each choice we make and each experience
we have, our perspectives change regarding much of what we hold
to be true. How many of us can say that we see our world and the
people in it the same way we did ten years ago, or five, or even
two? And the changes in the world around us are mind-boggling.
Newspapers, television, and bloggers can barely keep up with the

political, economic, and social changes that happen effortlessly each day around the globe. Change swirls around us in our modern world in unprecedented ways.

Often, the moment we feel we have a handle on life is the exact same moment when a curveball is thrown our way. We are forced to adapt, and that is never more true than when we face a crisis.

As I reflect on what it means to adapt to change, I am reminded of a frustrating experience I had as a young child. I will never forget the day—I had been working on a jigsaw puzzle for a very long time and I was nearly done with it. The picture had come to life before me, and I can remember the feeling of relief and accomplishment as I placed the last pieces. And then, just as I slid the final piece into place, a younger child came along, tearing through the room. Powerless, I watched in disbelief as the child destroyed my puzzle, leaving it in a heap on the ground.

How frustrating an experience for a young child! It is that much more frustrating for us as adults when we feel we have everything under control, things have finally come together, only to have them fall apart before our eyes. So often, we barely have time to sit back and appreciate our "completed puzzles" before someone or something comes tearing through the room of our life, turning things upside down. "I have put so much into developing this career and now it is taken away from me." "I have worked so long to save all this money, and now, within just a few months, I have lost most of it." In this life, we are constantly called to have courage and start over, patiently putting the pieces together again. Moreover, we must be willing to adapt when the puzzle itself changes, when we must abandon the pattern we have been following with its recognizable challenges in order to face entirely new landscapes.

The magnitude of change, and the speed with which it occurs within our economy, political system, careers, and the subsequent fallout in our personal lives is staggering. It is forcing a reconsideration of so much of what we have taken for granted. Times of crisis highlight this aspect of life that is always with us but is often subtle, gradual, and even imperceptible. Life is change. It is subtle and imperceptible no longer.

The experience of change has always rested at the center of our human experience and it can take us a long time to accept that these two things—change and being human—go hand-in-hand. Despite our knowledge of its inevitability, change has the unique capacity to sneak up on us. So often it feels like we cannot handle it, like it is impossible to "keep up." It is similar to the feeling we have when we say, "I try to take one day at a time, but sometimes it feels like several days hit me all at once." We may even find ourselves falling into snares of regret and disillusionment, wondering how we came to live the life we have. How often do we hear someone lament, "This marriage (or this career, this child, this *life*) is not what I expected!" Eventually we begin to realize that the unexpected is more the norm than what we planned for and we find all this difficult to accept. Change can leave us feeling so daunted that we simply want to run away from it all.

The real difficulty is the change that comes upon us from outside, not the change we initiate and freely choose. Change that is chosen by us can often be exhilarating and positive, and we rightly take great pride in it. The change created by our choices to marry, have children, pursue higher education, or embark on a new career can be very positive, resulting in a sense of personal fulfillment. But this is change that we orchestrate; we choose the time and place when it occurs. When change is imposed upon us it is an entirely different experience. It can leave us feeling out of control, fearful, even shake our sense of reality. This is what makes times of crisis so very difficult. This is the kind of change that rocks our understanding of who we are since we often define ourselves by our context: *I am married, I have this career, I am a student, I am young, I am healthy.* A drastic, unforeseen change can shatter our world: a loss of a job, miscarriage, illness, death, infidelity, all of which can change our world in a second. These changes are not chosen, asked for, desired, but are instead imposed upon us. We are left feeling insecure and wondering: *Who is in control here? Is life just a series of random occurrences? Is there any meaning to all this? Is my loss simply to be chalked up to bad luck?*

These are essentially religious questions leading us to consider whether there is another way of looking at change. I believe there is.

Similar to our longing for "more," the human experience of change may be saying something very positive and hopeful for us. If we are hardwired for change as the one constant in the human experience, then perhaps those earth-shattering changes that rock us to our core are actually opportunities for improvement and growth. Change reminds us that we have the potential to transform, to become more than we are, better than we are. Change can be the very energy in life that shows us that we are never completely limited by any situation or circumstance because we have within ourselves the capacity to become something new.

I believe this is what the great nineteenth-century theologian John Henry Newman was saying when he wrote: "To live is to change and to be perfect is to have changed often." By listening to the changes we experience in life we can learn something about ourselves, and in the process maybe even discover that we are not alone.

Without a spiritual perspective, losing a job is simply bad luck and the negative effects imposed upon us are seen as a series of closed doors that are unconnected and lead nowhere. But from another perspective, these occurrences are not all there is. It is possible that something will grow out of these events. They are connected, leading us to something better. At the very least these events lead us to a new examination of our lives and the consideration of a new way of living. Our path may be circuitous and seem to randomly go this way and that, but ultimately there is a general direction forward, if we listen to what these events are saying to us.

A wonderful example of this is the movie *Slum Dog Millionaire*. The movie begins with four statements from which we must choose:

1. He cheated.
2. He is lucky.
3. He is a genius.
4. It is written.

The main character, Jamal Malik, has led a very sad and tragic life. He is from the slums and his mother was killed by religious extremists when he was young. Later he is taken in by a group of adults that manipulate children for financial gain. After escaping from these adults he is forced to live on the streets by his own wits. Along the way he falls in love with a woman from whom he becomes separated, and he is desperately trying to find her. In the hope that she would see him on TV, he enters the Indian version of the television show *Who Wants to Be a Millionaire?* He surprises everyone by knowing the answerers to the questions. How is this poor, uneducated kid from the slums able to do this?

The movie reveals that the unique experiences of his life, most of them horrific and disastrous changes that wrenched his world in two, have given him the answers to the trivia questions, and by having the answers to the questions he is able to achieve his dream: find the woman he loves. The movie ends by giving the surprising answer: "It is written."

I would not suggest that any of the tragedies in his life were something we would wish for or that God intended for him, but I would suggest that even the very difficult experiences of life can speak to us, reveal something to us, even lead us somewhere very good. To say, "It is written" would suggest that there is a writer. That would mean one very important thing: We are not alone. There is someone or something involved in every occurrence of our lives, someone who is speaking to us, luring us to the grace and the presence of God even amidst the darkest and most unexpected events. It is as if God is writing something with us as we go through life, urging us to receive the grace that is provided along the way.

Another example of this is found in the movie *Cast Away* with Tom Hanks. Hanks plays Chuck Noland, a very important executive for FedEx, who is deserted on an island after the plane he is on crashes. Among the debris that has floated ashore are some FedEx boxes. Noland opens the boxes only to discover ice skates, video tapes, a little girl's ballerina outfit, and a volleyball he comes to call "Wilson." Initially these items look silly and useless to him and to the situation in which he finds himself, but as the movie progresses we discover that he actually ends up using all of these items to help him survive and escape. Noland was given what he needed.

The point is that we are all given what we need in life. The real issue is whether we are looking, listening, and open to discovering what it is—to recognize a very intimate God who is present in all human activity, who is trying to help us find what we are seeking. For Chuck Noland it was freedom. For Jamal Malik it was finding the woman he loves. If we are listening, even the seemingly mundane, the apparently un-god-like, and the negative circumstances of life, can reveal something of God's presence with us. This is the God of surprises, the one who comes where and when we least expect. This means something very wonderful: There are no "God-Free Zones." Everything can speak of the one who is with us, inviting us to see as God sees, the one who is the source and power for change that is available to all: rich and poor, learned and unlearned, young and old, even those who cannot afford to buy self-help materials. Someone who is available to all of us who know that things are not well enough and that there must be more, requiring only that we are open and listening. (But we must be open to it and listening for it.)

One thing both Jamal Malik and Chuck Noland have in common is that they both know what they want, what they truly desire more than anything else. This knowledge and desire was discovered, sharpened, and brought into clear focus by something else they also had in common: crisis. It is in the context of crisis that the clarity of what their lives are all about was discovered. It can be the same for us as well.

• • •

## PERSONAL REFLECTION

*Think of a time when you thought you had completed the puzzle of a part of your life, only to have it turned upside down. What did that experience do to you? What did you take away from it?*

# CRISIS

*"There, peeping among the cloud-wrack above a dark tor*
*high up in the mountains, Sam saw a white star twinkle*
*for a while. The beauty of it smote his heart, as he looked*
*up out of the forsaken land, and hope returned to him. For*
*like a shaft, clear and cold, the thought pierced him that in*
*the end the Shadow was only a small and passing thing:*
*there was light and high beauty forever beyond its reach."*
*~J.R.R. Tolkien, The Return of the King*

I N THE WORLD OF THE BIBLE, THE WORD CRISIS has two meanings. In the most familiar sense of the term, "crisis" refers to a cataclysmic upheaval; but the word crisis can also mean an opportunity, a moment filled with potential. The latter interpretation is quite different from what most of us may immediately think of, yet we know it is true from both our own experience and the experiences of others. All sorts of different crises can and have affected people and society, be it the loss of a loved one, an illness, a job loss, economic decline, social or interpersonal strife, addictions, divorce, war, natural disaster—the list goes on. But it is not the type of crisis that matters, but how those individuals or societies have responded to it that is so telling.

Some are destroyed by the crisis, while others discover a new and better life as a result. The destruction and unraveling of one's life due to a crisis is understandable. Life can be so very hard, and often we are faced with circumstances that seem beyond our capacity to cope. At the same time the human spirit can find within itself a stirring, a gathering of inner resources, and the strength to reevaluate assumptions and press forward in a new direction that is born out of, *and because of,* the crisis.

I often give retreats and missions and I like to ask people a clarifying question. "Where have you experienced the most growth, learning, and personal development in your life? Was it mostly from your successes, awards, and achievements, or from your failures, sufferings, and losses?" Invariably they say the latter. At the same time we all know that it is up to us to determine whether the outcome of our personal and societal crises will be positive or negative. The good news is that there is something within each of us, and the power of God for all of us, to make the outcome positive. Crisis can be the starting point for discovering this.

My journey within began in a rather dramatic way. My father died suddenly when his excessive working and drinking and his lack of personal care finally caught up with him. I was sixteen. The suddenness of it all was a shock. At first I was stunned and disoriented and quite fearful for my future and my family's. It was not long, however, before something else began to take place within me: a new, deep, and mature questioning of myself, life, and God. With an intensity that most sixteen-year-olds do not have, I began to assess the questions that arose as a result of the circumstances that had been forced upon me. *What is this life all about? What direction will I go with my life? Where is my father? Is there a God and a life after this?*

Looking back I am very grateful that I took that turn within and faced those challenging questions when I did. I know that not everyone in a similar situation does. It is possible, even in the face of death, to skim over the surface of it all and deny the questions so inherent in a painful experience. For me, this is when I believe *my life* began. It was no longer okay to "just go with the flow" and accept whatever was around me as all there was. Now I questioned and searched. My life began to feel more authentically my own. I was propelled by a crisis—and my direction in life would never be the same.

In a similar fashion, cultures and societies are challenged by great crises as well. It was not long ago that we rested securely in the belief that our military power would keep us safe and that violent acts of war and terrorism happened in other countries, but not in the United States of America. But now we know that even a small, seemingly insignificant group of terrorists can cause us serious harm, both in terms of the actual physical violence and the destruction of our sense of security.

It was not long ago that we rested secure in our belief in the growth of our economic system. Investments always increased in value and there would always be more money to help us buy what we wanted and needed, or so we thought. Now we know that is not the case, that the collapse of our economy can be a real possibility.

## LIFE IS ABOUT CHOICES

Sometimes crisis can be a positive thing. Of course we would never wish for the pain and hardship that it causes, but when we respond in the right way, crisis causes us to re-think our basic assumptions about what we can count on and where our true security is found. Like a sudden shifting of the tectonic plates beneath our feet, crisis causes huge realignments in our society, and where it will all end no one knows for sure.

In the midst of the difficulties and changes we are facing, we always have a choice. We have the choice to believe only in what we see before us or rather to consider new opportunities, to stretch our vision to see something new, not yet considered, a possibility of something more that is waiting to be discovered. And more often than not, we encounter this "something more" *because* of our uncertainty, not in spite of it. The potential for this to happen depends on our perspective and it begins with looking within and asking the big questions: Why am I here? Where am I going? What do I really want in this life and what do I really believe in? What are my strengths? Where am I free and where am I stuck?

Crisis can be the invitation to see more clearly and there is one crisis that cuts very deeply, one many have experienced: financial crisis.

## MONEY...AND LOSS

A young reporter once met an aging John D. Rockefeller sitting alone on a park bench. He asked, "Mr. Rockefeller, how much is enough money?" The elderly tycoon pondered the question for a moment and then with a tight smile replied, "Just a little bit more."

What strikes me so much about his response is not the obvious fact that one of the wealthiest men in human history would have said this (that motivation is probably a large part of why he became so rich). Rather, what strikes me is the possibility that Rockefeller speaks for all of us as well. To consider that our lives, in a subtle and even unconscious way, have been fashioned and patterned in much the same pursuit, is unsettling. At some level we have come to believe that our lives will be better, a "good" life, if only we had ___. We think, *Life will be better, and I will be better, when I have it. Just a little bit more. Having more means being more.* We all seem to agree.

We see this in our language. "He/she is successful and doing well." We have conflated "success" with money, and having money means we are "doing well." If we are honest with ourselves, we will see just how much we believe this. It is interesting to note that Jesus never says this in the gospels. He never equated success and well being with money. He actually says the complete opposite. But all around us are signs that our society has gone in the opposite direction. Just how tightly do we hold on to this belief?

I will never forget an experience in my life that caused me to personally confront that question. Having worked in the field of education all my professional life, I have never had an excess of money. In fact I had to work two jobs for many years to make ends meet. We always had enough, but not much extra, leaving me with little experience in the arena of financial investing. In 1999 my mother died, and I inherited a sum of money. I had known I would one day receive this money, and I had counted on it for my children's college education and my wife's and my retirement. Reading about financial planning convinced me that the most responsible thing for me to do was to invest this money so it could grow for our future needs.

I sought people's advice and settled on a very conservative investment group that toted their "safe" approach to investing. Their goal was not so much to grow the money quickly, but to maintain steady growth while not losing any of it in the process. After investing a sizable portion of my inheritance with this financial group, I felt I had done a prudent, wise, and safe thing. I went about my busy life not giving much attention to its development. After all, I was in it for the long run. After several initial months of success, the stock market turned sharply in a negative direction. I did not look too carefully into my investments since I knew the investment group was conservative and "safe." I waited too long.

When I finally did call, I discovered the funds had dropped considerably. I panicked and took my money out. I had lost forty percent of my principal investment.

I did not take the news well. I was more furious than I can ever remember being. I was so outraged at this investment firm that I had trusted and equally angry at myself. I felt like such a fool and a failure as a husband and father. We needed that money and I lost it. I stormed into the garage and began kicking boxes and using language that normally never comes out of my mouth. I proceeded to the basement and pounded my son's punching bag until I became exhausted. Afterwards I fell into a chair, physically spent, and filled with raw emotion. My mind was spinning wildly: What would I say to my wife? What would she say to me? I had never felt more vulnerable in my life as I did at that moment.

Then the phone rang. It was my wife. I didn't want to tell her and initially I avoided the topic, but she could tell something was wrong by the tone of my voice. "What is it?" she asked. I said nothing. She repeated the question. I knew I could not avoid this forever, so I told her. There was a pause, during which I could feel the stress and anxiety coursing through me. First, she said what I thought she might. "No one is sick; no one is in an accident. There are worse things." (That was very nice but it did not make me feel any better.) Then she said the words I will never forget. "Well, if losing that money helps you grow in faith, then how much of a loss was it?"

I was stunned. My racing thoughts and emotions were brought to an immediate halt. It was a moment of truth so penetrating that

I was temporarily disoriented by its clarity. It was like the moment a light is turned on when you have been lying in a darkened room. When the light is flipped on, you blink and quickly turn away because so much is revealed in an instant that you cannot take it in all at once.

My wife's statement was profoundly true, and I knew it the moment I heard it. It was a very rare opportunity for faith that was given to me, an opportunity to believe what I have said I believed: There is a God of love who knows me personally and whom I can trust with my life. I knew at that moment that I did not trust God the way I should. I knew at that moment how deeply my trust in money had penetrated my life. I was faced with a very difficult choice: to let the money go, to trust and believe in God's love, to believe that my self-worth was much more than this financial failure...or to stay stuck in my anger, resentment, and guilt.

There are few things as challenging to us as the loss of money. We are more like John D. Rockefeller than we would ever consciously admit, regardless of how much money we may actually have. Our deepest security is in what we own, what we have saved, our "securities" and "investments." To find our true security beyond money, to trust in something or someone more than money, really trust and not just give it lip service, brings us into a profound place of spiritual freedom. It means that we have meaning, value, and purpose even when we do not have money. It means living in a joy and freedom that no one can take away.

While I would never wish a financial crisis to happen to anyone, it does happen. Many people experience financial loss and uncertainty in their lives, and for many of us it is a true crisis and a very difficult experience indeed. At the same time, there is a great opportunity for reassessment and the shifting of our focus on what is most important in our lives. Do our lives remain a profound and unique gift even in the midst of economic loss? If not, then some spiritual "right-sizing" may be required.

What often precipitates a financial crisis, and is no less difficult, is a career crisis. Like all crisis it offers us the opportunity, once again, to see more clearly.

• • •

## PERSONAL REFLECTION

*What in your life do you desire "just a little bit more" of? Money, prestige, belongings? How is your drive for more of it affecting your life?*

# WHAT MATTERS

*"Where your treasure is, there your heart will be also."*
*~Matthew 6:21*

I F YOU WERE TO ASK A RANDOM GROUP OF PEOPLE fifty years ago what they considered to be the building block of society, family or careers, most all of them would probably have responded that it was the family. Sometimes I ask that same question to a random group of people today and the response is quite different: mixed, at best, and often with "careers" as the clear winner. In an exceptionally brief amount of time, we have shifted in our consciousness from a foundational belief in family to a greater belief in careers. This was driven home to me quite sharply one day.

I was driving to work and was listening to our local city radio news station. There came on the air a brief story reporting on the development of a new social trend. The report stated that this year the most common name given to newborn babies had changed in recent years. The report ended with the following statement: "The group compiling this data then went on to interview the parents of these children and ask them why they had chosen this name. The most common reply was, 'Because it would look good on their resume.'"

I was so shocked I had to pull the car over. From the time a child is born, the overwhelming consideration, before all else, is his or her career. No longer naming a child after a relative, a special person, or a saint, parents now want their children's names to look good on a piece of paper.

If achieving the career of your dreams with great success is the desire of your heart, and if you believe that to be the mission and the purpose of your life, then naming your baby for a resume makes sense. I only hope that you are honest with yourself and can confidently say that this is what you truly want more than anything else, not because someone else has put it in your head. The reason it is so important to understand what we truly value when it comes to our careers is that these career decisions will significantly impact our relationships with others. So much is required and demanded of us today to be successful in our careers that it is easy to get our values and perspective lost in the process.

For example, consider that we are all given a "psychic pie" each day. Our psychic pie is our emotional, physical, intellectual, and spiritual energy for that day. How and where we spend the pieces of that pie will tell us what we believe is most important. If we have eight slices of this pie and we spend seven and a half slices on the pursuit of our career, with only a half a slice left for our personal, relational, and spiritual life, then our lives will be unbalanced and our personal well-being, marriages, and friendships will suffer. To maintain healthy personal lives, to be physically, emotionally, and spiritually healthy requires an investment of our time and energy. It requires us to be fully present to that which we love and believe is most important to us, for if we are not, then these things are not important. It does not ring true when someone says, "My wife and children are the most important things in my life," if one has only the leftovers of life to offer them.

Building a career that we love and in which we excel can be a wonderful and productive aspect of life. However it still remains only *one* aspect of our lives and who we are. It is not the whole. If we overly identify ourselves with our careers, then the loss of a career can be life-shattering. Like the loss of money, the loss of a career can cut very deep. There are both good reasons for this and some not-so-good reasons. It is very difficult to lose a career that has given us a sense of satisfaction and meaning, a career that has enabled us to care for ourselves or our families. Again, I would not wish the loss of a career on anyone, but that does not stop it from happening. The end of a good career is a true loss, but it is one loss, not everything. It is everything only if we have made it into everything. When a radical change is imposed upon us we are once again profoundly challenged with the opportunity to reassess our lives, our focus, and our trajectory to see if we have strayed off course, perhaps unconsciously, from what is most important to us. Think of it this way: When you brace a ladder against a building, what is the goal you are trying to reach? Getting to the top of the building, or the climb up the ladder? The route is ultimately superfluous to the goal, so if one ladder won't make it to the top of the building, another one may do just as well.

I have a friend who is a psychologist and who spent many years in hospice counseling, working with patients who were dying and their families. He told me that in all those years he never heard anyone say, "My biggest regret is that I didn't work more/harder/longer hours" or, "I wish I had made more money." He worked with people who came from all over the economic spectrum and he never heard anyone regret how much money they had. Instead they wished they had spent more time with family and friends, or taken the time for themselves to grow as a person. The biggest regrets were always about relationships. These people in hospice care, at the ultimate point in human life, obtained great clarity about their lives, about what was most important and what was not. Perhaps it would be good to find this clarity long before we are dying?

I once heard someone say, "Nothing provides a better reason for reassessing life than a brush with death." There are many forms this brush with death can take. The loss of money or a career is a death of sorts, and it contains within itself an opportunity for clarity.

For many years I ran workshops for engaged couples preparing for marriage. I would always suggest to them that one of the greatest challenges to the success of their marriage will be the choices they make around their careers. I would add that there were no easy answers for them in this area. It would require hard and frequent dialogue, reviewing how the decisions in their careers were affecting their marriage so that one day they did not wake up as strangers to one another. A healthy relationship requires time, energy, and physical and emotional presence. To keep the relationship a priority is essential in marriage. When speaking with couples at the workshops, I would say that they could choose to stress their marriage for that extra money to buy the car or house of their dreams, but on the day it arrives they should give it a big hug and see if it hugs back. I said, "No, there is only one person in your life that can do that and he or she is sitting next to you, and that is irreplaceable." The sad truth of the matter is that when these couples leave this workshop it is most likely they will never again hear anyone say this to them.

This kind of assessment of our lives takes work, but it is worth it. Unfortunately it is often propelled by a crisis. I have spoken to people who are in the midst of losing everything. They have lost their job, their money, and some are on the verge of losing their marriage. These are often very ambitious people who have enjoyed financial and professional success, and they say to me, "I am learning so much right now in my life, more than I ever imagined. I am seeing things about myself, people, and what I want in my life more clearly than I ever have." How they are responding to their personal crisis in terms of how they think about it and the choices they are making in their daily lives makes all the difference.

## LIFE IS TOO IMPORTANT TO MISS

My wife went to see her doctor for a routine visit, but he found something very abnormal: a large ovarian tumor, one-and-a-half times the size of a baby's head. It looked like ovarian cancer, which has a very low survival rate, but they would not know for certain until they operated. Due to a holiday, we had to wait three days for the surgery. We had three young children at the time and our hearts ached for them. During those three days I discovered that there is a different way that you talk, a different way that you hold the person you love, and even a different way that you pray at times like that. Life took on a new clarity that was sharp, defined, and, in an odd way, beautiful. I saw what really mattered to me and what did not. I discovered a tenderness and a movement within my human heart that left me open in a way I have rarely ever experienced. I found myself going through my days with a profound consciousness, thoughtfulness, and prayerfulness that filled each waking moment. It was very rich, very deep, very good.

Gratefully the news was positive. It was not cancer. Afterwards I remember thinking to myself, *What is this experience saying to me? What is it teaching me? What took me so long to live like this? Will I be able to maintain this new focus and disposition that I have found to be so very rich?*

The short answer to that question is no. It is our human nature to become complacent when things are going well, and so that heightened awareness I felt during a time of family crisis naturally declined over time. I still try to recall it, however, when I feel that I am becoming too complacent, when I sense a spiritual inertia overwhelming me.

I think that most of us could benefit from the soul-searching that results from seriously pondering what matters most, yet few of us actually do. More importantly, how many of us change the way we live once we know what we want and value most in life?

Once we have answered those questions for ourselves, we can use that knowledge as a tool to help us in the decisions we make, the kinds of lives we create for ourselves, and to be true to ourselves and exhibit a sincere congruity between what we believe and how we act—our beliefs being reflected in our actions and how we live our lives. Of course, all of us slip in this. We say our spouses or children are the most important people in our lives, but place work priorities before family. We lose ourselves in busy-ness and distraction until we find little time and energy left for what we say we value the most. To be in touch with our deepest values and beliefs and to live accordingly would create an exceptionally rich and satisfying life because we would no longer waste our energy pursuing goals superfluous to what we value most in life. When I give retreats I often ask the following question to help people begin to answer this question for themselves:

If you were to go to the doctor and learn that you had six months to live, how would you spend those final months? How would you live your life? How would you look at the sunset? What would you say to those you love? What resentments would you let go (and which would you hold onto)? How would you pray? Again, sometimes crisis can be an opportunity for growth.

There is an exceptional quote from the sixteenth-century Spanish mystic Teresa of Avila that has helped me answer what matters most in my life:

*Remember that you have only one soul; that you have only one death to die; that you have only one life, which is short and has to be lived by you alone; and that there is only one glory, which is eternal. If you do this, there will be many things about which you care nothing.*

This statement is extraordinarily helpful for those of us trying to decipher our own personal meanings of life. Acknowledging the brevity of our lives and our ultimate deaths can be a wonderful tool to teach us how to live well, make the correct choices, and to find ourselves in the places in life where we truly want to be. Recognizing our lives as short and as ours alone to live gives us the freedom to see the things we really care nothing about and the things we care everything about. It gives us a particularly important and necessary clarity in the midst of crisis and uncertainty. If we are honest, we see how much we live the opposite, ignoring what we care the most about and fussing over the things we really care nothing for. Seeing what really matters makes all the difference. It gives us the insight and freedom to stand with a sense of security in who we are and what our lives are ultimately all about even in times of darkness and difficulty.

If we look within ourselves, what is it we discover that we care everything about? What do we want more than anything else? Knowing the answer to this question makes deciding the right choices in life relatively easy. It creates an energy, conviction, and willingness to work, risk, and even suffer. Our lives are grounded in a new way and energized like never before. We would no longer feel ordinary, and we would not live that way.

Nelson Mandela was a man of extraordinary clarity and conviction about what was most important to him. At his trial, when everyone knew the outcome before it began, in his closing words he said that ending apartheid "is an ideal which I hope to live for and to achieve. But if needs be, it is an ideal for which I am prepared to die." Imagine having the strength to weather the storms that life sends at us the way he did. When you have this kind of focus and clarity in what you believe in and want more than anything else in life, strength flows naturally. How else would he have had the stamina to endure decades in jail and never waver in his conviction in his mission? Even after his many years of imprisonment, he was able to remain a vibrant and positive force as he led his nation into reconciliation and unity. That is the kind of power that comes to us when we know ourselves and what we value more than anything else.

It is the kind of experience I had during those three days of waiting for the diagnosis of my wife's condition. It created within me a disposition of radical questioning and openness to something "out there" that was also so deeply within me as well. I knew during those days that I was not alone, and that was what I needed. These are moments of grace; as Augustine said: "You shouted, you broke through my deafness, you flashed, and dispelled my blindness."

If we are not alone, then that would make all the difference. It did for me.

• • •

## PERSONAL REFLECTION

*Take some time to really look deeply at yourself. What do you discover that you care everything about? What do you want more than anything else?*

# DECISIONS

*"In good times and in bad."*
*~Rite of Marriage, Catholic wedding vows*

I WILL NOT BEGIN TO PRETEND TO ANSWER the great mystery of human suffering, especially not the most difficult question of all: "Why do bad things happen to good people?" We have all asked this question when we have seen calamity strike those we love most. And most of us have asked ourselves a similar question in our own times of crisis: *Why is this happening to me?*

I will never forget what one young college student wrote in her academic journal when she reflected on this question:

*I can't believe what is happening to me. No matter how hard I try I am failing in two of my classes. A boy, who I had an incredible crush on, just told me*

*he is going back to his old girlfriend. Great. I have*
*just had an argument with my roommates, I'm*
*getting sick, and on top of all this, when I go home for*
*spring break I will be living for the first time with my*
*mother's new husband and his son, who happens to*
*be my ex-boyfriend. Days like today make me think,*
*"Why does it have to be so hard?" I feel like God is*
*punishing me for something, but I don't know what.*

No person is spared from suffering and we all find ourselves asking the question *Why?*

I do not believe we will ever receive the answers to all our questions in this life, but we can come to a place of acceptance with that reality. At the same time, what we do have within ourselves is the ability to choose, in the midst of our deep questions and confusion, how we will respond when we face the crises that life brings our way. On the cross Jesus, the human Jesus, knew abandonment and despair, yet still he chose to continue to trust. We, too, always have a choice, and this is where the transforming power of faith comes into play.

One thing is for certain: that God does not control us or orchestrate the intricate details of our lives. We are not puppets on a string, nor is God the great Puppeteer who pulls on the strings of our lives, creating some cosmic play. God does not dictate how our lives will end up, doling out rewards to some and punishments to others, for that would negate the greatest gift God ever gave humanity: free will. Faith would lose its meaning and power. Instead, faith is rooted in love—God's love for us and our love for God. Love, in its true sense, must be freely chosen. If love is manipulated or controlled, if it is based on fear or coercion, then it is not love. At the same time, it must be true that God does participate in the events of our life precisely because that is also the nature of love. Love is not removed from the one it loves; instead, it is involved and present.

To understand how we can make this connection with God, I would like to suggest the analogy of a healthy marriage. Healthy marriages are freely chosen, not only on the wedding day but each day of life thereafter. The free choice to love one another each day is what creates a "living sacrament," a place where God resides. This divine presence is revealed and made manifest through and in the daily choice to love the other "in good times and bad, in sickness and health, till death do us part." Those remarkable words couples say on their wedding day and pledge to live every day thereafter are mighty words that should make us pause reverently before the extent of their meaning. We would only require a brief moment of self examination to acknowledge our limited capacity to love in such a way. The good news is that is precisely where God comes in. Divine love, in which our human loving partakes, has been given to us for every moment of our lives, especially in our moments of weakness and inadequacy. The choice is always ours, to do it alone or to be open to divine love, to another "person" of love who is with us at the center of each moment of our lives.

All marriages experience periods of disillusionment. "This is not what I expected." "I didn't sign up for this." "He/she is not the person I thought they were." In marriage we discover things about the other we were never fully aware of on our wedding day. In short, we are surprised.

When we marry it is normally because of the beauty, uniqueness, and special qualities we find in the other person. If we are in a healthy marriage and stay in it long enough, working hard for its success, we will discover two things. First, that the other person is more beautiful and unique than we ever realized. Second, that the other person is more broken and imperfect than we ever realized. We are given the privilege to see the other person the way God sees. We see the beauty and the brokenness, and we are left with the question: Do we run away or embrace the other person? If we embrace the broken part of the other then true union is possible. This is similar to the love God shows for humanity. God embraces all of the beauty and all of the ugliness of our human reality without condition. A healthy marriage mirrors on a personal scale the universal love that God has for humanity. It is one way in which we encounter the divine and discover the one who is "out there" and who is within us—the one we call God.

Much like how we react to crises in our lives, it is how we respond to these revelations in our relationships that is most critical.

During times of disillusionment many marriages come to an end. Alternatively, this is precisely when other marriages truly begin, starting with the choice to love and work at loving the other when everything within does not feel like doing so. To love sacrificially, to love for the good of the other and the good of the relationship, is to love the way God loves us. By loving in this way we enter into God and meet God in the circumstances of our life. A sacrament occurs in our midst, often subtle and initially unrecognizable. As time goes on we begin to see the redemptive power of this way of loving. It begins, in a nearly imperceptible way, to turn all things for the good because we have allowed the grace of God's love to reside in our choice to love.

In the Hebrew Bible God's love is revealed as "Hesed" love: unconditional, committed, covenant love that never ends. In the New Testament God's love is revealed in the self-sacrifice of Jesus' life for all of humanity, his extension of mercy without condition. When we love in these ways, we enter into the life of God. Suffering is somehow transformed, and a new dimension opens.

Jesus' parable of the Good Samaritan profoundly illustrates this way of acting in love and mercy. It is worth retelling here:

A man had been robbed, beaten, stripped, and lay on the side of the road, bleeding and near death. Initially, several religious people come by, each passing on his way, ignoring the man on the road. They convinced themselves of the prudence and righteousness of their inaction. It was risky to stop for someone on this road because outlaws sometimes waited in ambush. Additionally, for the Jews, it was an "unclean" act to touch the blood of another. It was not until a Samaritan, a people whom the Jews despised and considered ungodly, came by that mercy was shown on the poor man. The Samaritan risked his own safety and bandaged the injured man's wounds, put the man on his own donkey, took him to an inn, paid for his care, and returned to follow through on the man's recovery.

What the Samaritan did was so remarkable because of the hatred between the Jews and Samaritans. Jesus told this story to show that we are all neighbors, despite our differences. The Samaritan epitomizes the best of humanity, as seen in his actions and his choices, even if the injured man was conscious of it or not.

This is the essence of what we do in marriage (as well as in friendship, familial love, and sometimes to the stranger we meet on the road). When we marry we see all that is "well" with the other. It is only later that we discover their wounds. In marriage we stop our life—get off our horse—and invest our time, our money, and follow through in the care of the other. We change our life and take a considerable risk in doing so. When we embrace the wounds of the other, we live a life of faith in the One who embraces all of our wounds. Love is as love does. Faith is as faith does. All the challenges of this human life are opportunities to love God, self, and others—or not to. To love in such a way reveals a certain trust in the one who walks with us. The character and dimension of our love and faith in times of crisis, worry, and uncertainty reveal and deepen, and even create within us, a new reality of love and faith. To trust that the mysterious movement of divine grace is at work, particularly during these times, is an act of faith to which we are continually invited. And it is an act that makes all the difference.

When you see a healthy, loving marriage (not a perfect marriage, as they do not exist), you will see something quite remarkable: imperfect people choosing to love "for better or for worse, in sickness and in health." These marriages are not conflict-free. Often they have more than their fair share of losses, crises, and worries, but the two people involved face those adversities with the power of human choice and the power of faith. The choice to love and look beyond the circumstances to the mysterious presence of the One who chooses to love us is what makes life "work" for these people. The bad news of life is often transformed into Good News by the mystery of the grace of God's love that is present in all the news of life. Even when it does not appear that all things are working for the good, people of faith trust in what they do not see because they have "seen it" in the past.

For example, I know a couple that has been married for twenty-eight years. During this time they have experienced several periods of unemployment, a few of which were long and financially devastating. The struggle and pressure they experienced in their marriage was deep and profound (as anyone who has experienced this knows well). To help them make it through these times, they decided to perform a simple daily act. Each day they would take a moment to stop whatever they were doing, look into each others eyes, and ask, "Are we okay today?" They would both reply, "Yes." They did not view this beautiful expression of love, even at times when they could see all the pain, fear, and worry, as a denial of the suffering they were experiencing, but as a way of sharing it together and still expressing their faith. No matter what was going on, they still had each other. By saying "Yes," they affirmed this, and at the same time affirmed together their trust in God, whom they believed was with them even more closely in their pain.

This "lived faith" is a profound act of belief and it creates a connection with God even in the most difficult of times.

Regardless of our state in life, married or single, we all live the same human condition. We all have to face what life sends our way, especially that which is unwelcome. "Life on life's terms," as they say in Alcoholics Anonymous. When we choose to love God in our decision to love the other, we are making a choice in how we are responding to that which is thrown at us. To choose to believe and trust in the hidden presence of divine love, through how we respond to the circumstances we encounter, will reveal a power to face the very struggles, challenges, and crises of human life head-on. It is living in this discovery—the discovery that we are not alone—that makes all the difference.

## THE CHOICES WE MAKE

Suffering, as well as happiness, occurs as a result of the change that is constantly happening all around us, whether or not we are aware of it. Those results depend on how we react to that change—the choices that we make.

A series of "minor" decisions weave together to create the direction of our lives and the realities that we face. When crisis and change confront us (suddenly we realize our marriage is on the rocks or company downsizing leaves us out of a job), we have the power to direct where our lives go from there and the type of people we become.

Augustine had a saying regarding the directions we take with our lives that has helped me and many others. Essentially he says, "A lame person going in the right direction makes more progress than a sprinter going the wrong way." Of course there are those who by fortune and circumstance appear to be sprinting through life, and we have our own fair share of limits and liabilities, but the real issue is this: *What kind of person am I becoming with what I have been given?*

We have all seen highly talented, gifted people who have been given so much in their lives yet nevertheless end up in very bad places. No one wakes up one day and says, "What can I do today to make a mess of my life?" even though that may be exactly what happens. The progress we make and the people we become are created through our choices, choices that may seem infinitesimal and of no significance. Christ tells us that "whoever is faithful in a very little is faithful also in much." It is our daily choices and responses to the changes in our lives, which may appear small and seemingly inconsequential, that build up within us, like a bank account in which we make deposits with our positive choices. Turning crisis and change into opportunities for positive transformation requires that we wake up each morning and reaffirm our commitment to the choices necessary to creating that transformation.

• • •

## PERSONAL REFLECTION

*Can I recognize how a series of seemingly small choices has created my life and led me to either a good or bad place?*

# GOOD NEWS, BAD NEWS... WHO KNOWS?

*"All things work together for good for those who Love God."*
*~Romans 8:28*

Y EARS AGO I CAME ACROSS A PROFOUND STORY that has comforted and challenged me regarding my perspective on loss and faith like no other. It is a story by Anthony DeMello:

*In a distant land there was an elderly man who lived in the countryside. One day his son captured a wild horse. All those around him said, "That is Good News," to which the elderly man replied, "Maybe." The next day the horse escaped. Everyone said, "We are sorry. That is Bad News," to which the elderly man replied, "Maybe." It turned out that the horse was the leader of a herd and returned to the stable with the entire herd of*

*horses. All those who witnessed this exclaimed, "What
Good News!" Once again, the man replied, "Maybe."
Later that week the man's son was attempting to
tame one of the wild horses and was thrown to the
ground and broke his leg. Everyone said, "That is Bad
News," to which the elderly man replied, "Maybe."
Several weeks later the army entered the village and
conscripted all the young men for a fierce battle that
was soon to take place. Seeing the man's son with a
broken leg, they left him behind. Everyone exclaimed,
"That is Good News." Finally, the elderly man said the
following: "Good News, Bad News.... Who Knows?"*

How do we perceive the "Bad News" of our lives? All of us
have had the experience of initially judging some occurrence in
our life, or in the life of one we love, as bad news only to realize
in retrospect that the perceived bad news ended up becoming
very good news. How often have we heard someone say: "If I
hadn't been fired from that job, I never would have left it and I
would not be where I am today;" or "I once thought I could never
live without that person, but I have grown and learned so much
about myself since that relationship ended. Now I an engaged to
the person of my dreams and I would not be here today without
that pain in my past."

In looking back on our lives we can all recognize events that initially looked good or bad but played out very differently in the long run. This reality has rung so true in my own life that I am reluctant to quickly judge events or situations as "good" or "bad." Often my wife and I will say to one another, especially when we are tempted to fall into a negative reaction to a perceived downfall, "Remember honey, 'Good News, Bad News.... Who Knows?'" Each time I hear this it is almost like a moment of grace, an invitation to faith, asking me if I really believe that something or someone else is at work in my life and that I am not alone on this journey. I sense the subtle presence of the divine that is manifested in the very events of my life when I choose to look beyond the surface for the potential of something more to be revealed.

Things sometimes have a way of working themselves out for the good in our lives but there is no guarantee. How we respond to the supposed bad news, however, will greatly affect whether or not it stays that way. Each piece of bad news, like every crisis and failure, is an invitation to choose either despair and inertia, or trust and action. Oftentimes the action demanded in response to the crisis is the very thing that is so personally transformative, setting the stage where we might grow in faith. Through the countless ways we respond, particularly in times of uncertainty, we access the divine presence and grow into people of faith.

If there is someone with us in this life, someone we can trust even when all is looking pretty bleak, just who is it then? How do we access this "someone?" Just how much "Good News" is there for us?

I think we begin slowly, by looking around us. As Yogi Berra once said, "You can observe a lot just by watching."

## TOO GOOD TO BE TRUE?

On warm summer evenings when I was young, I used to lie on the grass and look up at the stars. From time to time there would be a moment when my mind would halt its endless parade of youthful thoughts and I would find myself in silence, without and within. Looking up, I would gaze upon something so great, so much bigger than myself, and far more beautiful. It was a moment, often very brief, of pure wonder. My mind lost its bearings and I was present before something that bordered on utter mystery. I think these evenings under the stars were my earliest spiritual experiences.

As an adult I have sometimes found myself looking up at the stars, this time lying back on a lounge chair. Once again, from time to time, I have experienced that familiar moment: The chatter of my mind stops, my world becomes silent, and that sense of awe returns. Yet as an adult, I notice something new appearing as well: A creeping fear, a hidden and suppressed terror, begins to emerge. In recognizing what I am looking at, I am forced to admit the very real possibility of my complete and utter insignificance.

Blaise Pascal writes, "The eternal silence of these infinite spaces fills me with dread." When I experience this sense of being "filled with dread," I also begin to feel something else emerge. It's like a tug in another direction, a tug urging me to believe that even before the world and its majesty were created, *I mattered*. What's more, somehow there is a reason for me to trust that *I still matter.* My mind can lose its bearings and for a moment I can be present within a great mystery—and when this happens, I have to make a choice:

Does my life have true meaning and purpose, or not?

When gazing at the stars, this is no easy choice! These two options regarding my significance both loom before me, equally possible but with startlingly different consequences—one so magnificent, and one so horrid. On the one hand, there is the genuine possibility, in the light of this cosmos, that I am utterly and completely insignificant, nothing more than a tiny, infinitesimal life form floating in the vastness of the universe. And on the other hand, there is a chance that my existence in this world is significant and deliberate, in which case I would be touching upon a wonder more marvelous than I ever imagined possible. How do I decide? Do I choose to believe in something or someone beyond my understanding that allows me to make sense of my existence, that gives my life meaning? Or do I choose to believe that I matter nothing beyond this moment in time?

Whatever my answer is to these questions, one thing I know for sure is that the stars above me continue to force the issue and it is big. My question ultimately needs an answer, and the answer is grander than I can comprehend.

You see, as an adult I have come to learn things about the stars I never even dreamed of as a child. Now I know the following:

- The speed of light travels at 186,000 miles a second.

- That is 671,000,000 miles an hour or 5.9 trillion miles a year.

- The closest star to earth is Alpha Centauri. It is 4.3 light years away. (A light year is the distance light travels in one year, so traveling at the speed of light, it will take 4.3 years to reach our closest star.)

- The average distance between stars is 30 trillion miles, or just over 5 light years.

- The average galaxy has 100 billion stars, and in the universe, there are an estimated 100 billion galaxies.

- Some distant galaxies are 3 billion light years away from us.

- There are at least 100 billion stars in the Milky Way galaxy alone.

- The total number of stars in the known universe, according to a study by Australian astronomers, is 70,000 million, million, million (70 sextillion). That is about ten times as many stars as grains of sand on all the world's beaches and deserts.

When I look at the puffy, pinkish-white picture of a distant galaxy and I reflect on the millions of stars it represents, and when I couple that knowledge with the understanding of just how far away it all is, I actually get weak in the knees. It is all too much, almost impossible to wrap my mind around. It bears on us, weighs on us; it may even, in a sense, call out to us, to think in a new way, as we move about beneath the stars.

We have been given, in a single gesture, both an enormous privilege and an enormous challenge. We were born with the enormous privilege of knowing all this about the universe we find ourselves in—the privilege of knowing something so grand that no prior people even dreamed or dared to consider possible. Along with that privilege comes the enormous challenge in how we think about ourselves and how we think about God. This awareness of what surrounds us can truly change everything. In the light of the cosmos, our very existence, our assertions about life, and whatever we say about God, must begin as magnificent understatements. We do not possess the words that would even begin to scratch the first truth of faith in light of this knowledge. We are often torn between two thoughts when we ponder what surrounds us. One, that anyone would be a fool to believe in the possible existence of a God of this magnitude, that personal meaning and encounter with such a cosmic God is possible. Or two, that anyone would be an utter fool *not* to believe that the sheer complexity, scale, and beauty of the universe would not require the presence of God.

Attempting to answer either of these questions requires so much time and energy that many people have given up trying. This has led to a great tragedy that has taken place in our modern society and among the many expressions of Christianity and other religions. Instead of truly pondering God's presence in the universe, many of us have simply accepted God's presence and then relegated it to a convenient corner of our lives.

Instead of "dumbing down" our notions of God, we need to "think it up," turning up the wonder, basking in the mystery. Instead of thinking, *This is all too much, too good to be true,* consider that it just may be this good, this wonderful, this magnificent. This is why the tradition of faith has always had its prophets, those who cry out in the wilderness to keep us from settling for less, from attempting to contain that which cannot be contained.

Through our rational and idle pondering, we have rendered God and faith so small, manageable, and controlled—and thus, ineffectual. God and spirituality have become more like a source of personal improvement, and many strains of Christianity a do-it-yourself guide to salvation. The mystery of faith has been reduced to a set of answers to moral questions avoiding complexity and human struggle. More often today faith becomes just an extension of ourselves, our culture, our limited understanding, and our personal needs and wants. For so many of us, God is just about feeling good, giving us some temporary and vague reassurance in the face of the difficulties in this life and our impending death. In some religious circles God is even reduced to being the source of material and economic prosperity. This is an attitude toward faith that certainly fits well in our capitalist, consumer culture. God is seen primarily as a source of blessing, and that "blessing" is primarily financial in nature. For example, God can bless you with a better job, a better career, and more money, not to mention a very nice house. These blessings will come about if you have a good attitude and think positively about yourself and your life. It's easy to see how this perspective on faith plays very well in the United States. It is essentially the American dream that now has God as its sponsor. Too often we reduce God and faith to a checklist that notifies us when we have all our bases covered. In the same way as one would say, "I belong to the club, I have paid my dues, I am covered," we may think to ourselves, *I go to church, I give some money, I made a commitment of faith once, I am covered.*

To this I quote Tom Brady: "There's gotta be more than this." When we consider the mystery of the God of the cosmos, how utterly amazing, grand, and exciting the journey of faith in this God must be. The problem is that it is our human instinct to make God an extension of ourselves. Making God comfortable to us allows us to stay in control, and control is a powerful human desire—even though it is the very desire to control that gets us in the most trouble in life and in our faith. When we try to control God, we are choosing to see the Creator of the Universe through the bias that we, the creation, have made. This artificial understanding toward

God allows us to believe that the nature of God is exactly as we want it to be or as we have come to perceive it to be.

We see this all the time in human relationships. A spouse wants their partner to be a certain type of person, or to act the way he/she did when they first met. Parents want their children to pursue a certain type of career and not be the unique individual they are. I remember coming home from college for the holidays to be with my family. By that time I had lived for a year in Europe and had many new perspectives on life. I had grown and matured in numerous ways. However it became quite apparent that my family still thought of me as the person they remembered and would relate to me in the same way they were accustomed to—as their "little" brother or child. It was so frustrating, I wanted to shout, "Hey, this is me, a new person, an adult, different. Don't you see?"

In the same way, we try to compartmentalize God and make our experience with the divine convenient for us. We pull God out on Sundays or for the occasional sacramental celebration, just to shove God away until we decide we want the presence of the divine again. I think the only way out from this limited understanding and approach to God and into a more genuine faith and belief is to listen with effort and humility, to take a closer look at what we say we know to be true.

Indeed, we drastically limit our notion of God when we do not look around us. If we take the time to be mindful, to really encounter what we have been given the opportunity to see, our experience would never allow us to limit God the way we do. We would experience a conversion of heart and intellect, a letting go of biases, class conditioning and insulation. It would imply an openness to learn, an appreciation of complexity, and, most important, a new humility. But sadly, many of us choose to think about the universe not as it is but rather in the same way medieval people did: God is above in the clouds waiting for us. In doing so we drastically reduce God and we simply miss out on so much of what it would be to experience the God of this immense grandeur. How much "more" must there be if this is the one who walks with us and who waits for us?

If there is a God who is reflected in the majesty of this universe, then we live within a reality that is so grand and so mysterious that the only proper place to begin on the journey of faith is profound awe.

The poet Edward Young said: "Too low they build, who build beneath the stars." I would have to add:

Too low we speak of God,
    we who speak of God beneath the stars.
Too low we pray,
    we who pray beneath the stars.
Too low we believe,
    when we believe beneath the stars.
Too low we think of ourselves,
    when we think of ourselves beneath the stars.

How we would struggle to find words when we spoke of God beneath the stars. How mighty and encompassing our prayers would be and what bold faith would pray them! Imagine the new confidence filling us, even during times of crisis. Imagine what it would be like to trade our worry for trust. God invites us to live with the most remarkable disposition: "Do not worry about your life.... Is not life more than food?.... And can any of you by worrying add a single hour to your span of life?.... But strive first for the kingdom of God and his righteousness, and all these things will be given to you as well." Matthew 6:25-34

What if we believed the biblical revelation that there is a God, and the first biblical statement that God is creator of this universe, and that every speck of this cosmos, every speck of our lives, is filled with God's presence? Then we would indeed walk the journey of this life, even in times of crisis, uncertainty, and worry very differently. Imagine the possibility, the good news, of the more yet to be discovered. Yes, it sounds too good to be true, but what if it is true?

• • •

## PERSONAL REFLECTION

*Take some time to ponder the vastness of the universe. How do you feel? What is it saying to you?*

# WHY AM I HERE?

*"Men go abroad to wonder at the heights of mountains,*
*at the huge waves of the sea, at the long courses of the rivers,*
*at the vast compass of the ocean, at the circular motions of*
*the stars, and they pass by themselves without wondering."*
*~St. Augustine*

**L**OOKING AT THE REALITY OF THE COSMOS for even a short time is challenging, to say the least. Our minds cannot take it all in; rather, we find ourselves barely mentally scratching at the surface, saying, "This is too much, why bother with this at all?" The only answer is because this is the reality that surrounds us, our reality, and reality speaks. All reality is worthy of listening to and pondering. The movement of all healthy faith begins first of all with patient listening, even if it is difficult to do so. Just as a person cannot be heard or understood unless another is truly listening, so too it must be for allowing God to speak. Listening to what we were born into rather than that which we wish we were born into is a good place to start. The very fact that we were born and exist may in fact say very much, if we listen. We may begin with the most fundamental of all questions, "Why am I here?"

In light of the cosmos, this question is daunting to say the least, and most who bother to ask it tend to draw one of two basic conclusions. Each is difficult to come to, and they are challenging for very different reasons—and with very different consequences.

## CONCLUSION ONE: OUR COMPLETE AND UTTER INSIGNIFICANCE

To put it bluntly: We are cosmically infinitesimal forms of life, clinging to a speck of cosmic dust. We have come about by evolutionary chance. We hit the cosmic jackpot! We will return to the dust upon which we live. The growth in prominence of the atheist movement in the new millennium is built upon this conclusion. At its best, this conclusion provides the motivation to end war, cure disease, and create world peace because it is truly up to humanity, and within humanity's capacity to do such things. If the universe came to be purely by natural laws and processes, then humanity can eventually come to fully understand those laws and harness their power for the benefit of everyone. It is simply a matter of learning how. At its worst, however, this conclusion justifies greed, reckless ambition, and disregard for our fellow persons because, in the end, none of it matters anyway.

## CONCLUSION TWO: OUR COMPLETE AND UTTER SIGNIFICANCE

I will need a little more allowance to explain this conclusion.

I was in high school when the mystery of my life began to take hold on the radar screen of my mind. I was speaking to my Dad's army friend from World War II and he casually mentioned that my father was seriously dating a woman from Texas during the war. He went on to say that he genuinely expected my father to marry that woman and he was very surprised to learn that he had instead met my mother, whom he wed in France during the war.

After hearing this story, a thought entered my young mind like a slap in the face: *What do you mean, 'marry this other woman?' What if he never met my mom? Where would I be? Would I even 'be' at all?"* From there, my mind began to spiral: *What if there hadn't been a war, or what if he had been assigned somewhere else? What if they had never met? And what if they married but somebody had a headache and they weren't together sexually the night I was conceived? Where would I be? Would I 'be' at all?* More questions came like rapid fire, touching upon my parents' parents and their parents until the fact that I was born at all started to appear so random that it seemed almost impossible.

Scientific insight adds to this mystery. There are about 50 million-400 million sperm cells present in each sexual act, and each sperm carries a different outcome, a different genetic code, a different life. A woman's egg comes approximately once a month, and it, too, has its own genetic code. So what is the chance of one particular sperm meeting one particular egg? How many fertilized eggs fail to implant in the uterus? How often does a pregnancy end through a miscarriage or abortion, and in the history of the world how many births ended in the death of the child while it was still very young? (Historically speaking, one-third to one-half of all children died at birth or when very young.)

So the chances of any particular person being born are so ridiculously low that to view it as a complete accident ignores the incredible reality that we are alive at all, and therefore our mere existence is evidence that we are very special and very significant creatures.

Alternatively we can look at our being here on this earth as an invitation into another mystery: *The mystery that I am.* My life is such an extraordinary exception, and therefore such a profound privilege, that to exist at all is an extraordinary statement in itself with profound consequences. To be sitting here reading this book, thinking these thoughts, at this moment in history, may be in and of itself the most profound statement of the reality and presence of God that there is. That I am here, that we are here, is a mystery that changes everything and points us to so much more. All our statements about ourselves do not even begin to catch the significance they attempt to communicate. We exist, and to exist at all is big. We are fortunate beyond comprehension and beyond measure. We have the opportunity of life, simply given to us, as gift, and that is magnificent.

. . .

Cosmic chance? Or divine intention? As Albert Einstein put it, "There are two ways to live: You can live as if nothing is a miracle; you can live as if everything is a miracle." Perhaps we are the miracle of God, a miracle intended for all time. Mother Teresa said, "Not every act of sexual intercourse is divine...but every conception is." What if that is true? Every conception has divine origin and shares in divine life. The mystery of our existence points to the mystery of God that fills the cosmos and holds all life in the Life of God, the one who is the Source and Giver of All Life. Abraham Heschel put it this way: "Just to be is a blessing. Just to live is holy."

I realized this truth personally at the birth of our first child. My wife and I had decided to have a natural childbirth. We went to the classes, learned about breathing, counting, and coaching. Now my wife is a nurse practitioner and the second oldest of nine children, and she has been around hospitals and babies long before her own pregnancy. I, on the other hand, am the youngest of three. I had never set foot in a hospital, never been around babies, childbirth, or even a pregnant woman.

You can imagine how this went.

When we arrived at the hospital, we discovered that my wife would be giving birth near the rooms of two other women, also our doctor's patients, who were in the late stages of childbirth. I remember walking down the hall and hearing the sounds that women make during childbirth coming from these adjacent rooms. I had never heard noises like this before. Once I realized what they were the thought seriously crossed my mind, *Perhaps it would be best if I just turned around and left my wife to the care of others.* I was so out of my element and knew right from the beginning that I would be treading water from here on out.

My wife's labor progressed quickly to match the pace of the other two women in labor. At one point, our doctor came in, checked my wife, and looked over at the nurse, saying, "You may have to do this one," before he rushed back out the door.

*What?* I said to myself. *Just this nurse and me? This is not going to happen!*

To make a long story short, I was useless. Breathing? Counting? Forget it. Pictures? Didn't get them. I was a waste, and much of the day was a blur. I must have been quite a sight with my eyes bugging out, my mouth wide open, and a look of panic on my face. Yet in the midst of this whirlwind, something happened. There was this moment, just after my daughter was born, when she was placed in my arms and time stopped. I held the most beautiful child in the world. I heard nothing, I was enveloped in silence and I received the moment of revelation. I held a miracle, I held a mystery, I held a life intended for all time by a Love that knows no time. A life that was held in the arms of real Love—held not only in my arms, but in the eternal arms of God. There was something sacred here, something divine. This was a truly spiritual moment for me and it was one that I will never forget.

I realized that day at the birth of my daughter that I was participating in God's work. In all the weakness and limitation of my humanity, I was participating in the creation of another human. If God is the creator, then I was participating in this activity of God. What a privilege, what an extraordinary exception my life is to be able to give life. Not only am I a miracle because I exist, my life is meant to be about miracles, participating in the thing that only God can do—create life, in all the many diverse and remarkable ways we are able to give life to others

This is the same insight a mother in the Old Testament has when confronted with her mortality and the mortality of her own children:

> *I do not know how you came into being in my womb.*
> *It was not I who gave you life and breath, nor I who*
> *set in order the elements within each of you. Therefore*
> *the Creator of the world, who shaped the beginning of*
> *humankind and devised the origin of all things, will in*
> *his mercy give life and breath back to you again.... I*
> *beg you, my child, to look at the heaven and the earth*
> *and see everything that is in them, and recognize*
> *that God did not make them out of things that existed.*
> *And in the same way the human race came into*
> *existence. Do not fear. (2 Maccabees 7:22-3, 28-9)*

Every parent who has held their newborn child knows something of the mystery reflected by this mother. Parents have those moments, even if very fleeting, when they touch upon the realization of something bigger than themselves—the one who is "out there" waiting for them and who at the same time is "in here," living within.

· · ·

## PERSONAL REFLECTION

*Think about yourself as a miracle and your very existence as the most profound statement of the reality and presence of God. How does this affect how you see yourself? How does it affect your outlook on those around you?*

# PART II

# HE HAS A NAME.
# IT IS JESUS.

*"The Word became flesh and lived among us."*
*~John 1:14*

A FRIEND OF MINE NAMED SAM LIVED MOST OF his early life without faith. He found himself one day on the beach, looking at the ocean and pondering the message of faith he had recently been invited to consider. He suddenly saw the vastness of it all. (The ocean is such a good place for this, with a drop of water in your hand and the ocean before you, picking up a speck of sand and seeing the beach upon which you stand.) He thought about the magnitude of the Christian message and wondered in the silence of his heart, *What if this is true? This story? What if this is true?* What happened next was the moment of faith. He said to himself, *Oh \*#&%, it is true!* Then he said the words that struck me so. "This changes everything." Indeed it would. It is in turning to the Christian story that we discover another way to understand all that we have been discussing and at the same time discover greater, even more startling possibilities for our lives.

Christian revelation is this: The God of the Cosmos was knit in a mother's womb, became a fetus, gestated, and was born in the pain of natural childbirth. The God of the Cosmos suckled at a mother's breast and needed a father to protect him. He grew "in wisdom and in years, and in divine and human favour" (Luke 2:52) and was obedient to his parents. He ate and slept, knew the pangs of hunger, and the taste of a good meal. Our God knew the heat of the sun, the ache from walking, the feel of dirt beneath his feet, the moisture of sweat pouring down his brow, the dryness of his mouth, the refreshment of a cool drink, and the comfort of sleep. He knew the wind in his hair, the taste of salt water, the smell of fish. He wept tears of sadness, and knew the joy of being utterly happy.

God was born here on this earth as a Jewish boy. He was born into an oppressed class of people on the outskirts of the Roman Empire in an obscure place in the distant past. Trained in the craft of carpentry, he lived with an assortment of people, most of whose reputations were questionable. He knew the comfort of friends, and equally understood what it was like to walk into a room where everyone despised him, knew what it was like to stand alone, to be unpopular and unappreciated. He experienced the embrace of children, the joy of their loving presence as well as the jeers of those who wanted nothing to do with him. Often he would sit at table with those who were most hated in the world, the socially unfit. He seemed most at home when he was with them and indicated that this revealed something of God, a God who is especially attentive to those most alienated, alone, broken, and despised—this is the One who walked this Earth many years ago.

The Christian story can be summed up as this: The God of the Cosmos has a name, it is "Jesus." The Christian faith is in a person, Jesus. He was God who took on human flesh. This is a grand statement, one that seems completely and utterly outlandish. St. Paul said that for the Greeks, this belief in Jesus is nonsense, and for the Jew, it is scandalous. On both accounts, the Greeks and the Jews are right: It makes no sense and it is scandalous to say that God, the Creator of all that is, became one of *us*. No other religion makes this claim, and with good reason. This Christian belief is truly preposterous, it is pure audacity at its fullest...and yet Christians believe it, and they make no apology for it.

This belief, if true, means that in some seemingly obscure but real way, we have been given a glimpse into the very nature of the God of the Cosmos. This God has come to us and is now accessible in a way no one could imagine possible. God, Creator of everything, Creator of all we know to be true, has become one of *us*. He has a face, a name, a history on this planet. He has spoken with us and lived among us. He *became* one of us. Indeed, Jesus shared in humanity with his own genetic code, so similar to all of the human race, yet different enough to create a unique person. The stuff of our humanity is now imbued with the very presence of God.

This changes everything. It changes how we view our very selves as human beings. One would rightly say, "I am a Christian, so I can be human." Imagine the humanity that is possible for one who understands him/herself this way. What greatness and what dignity we have when we see ourselves as having been given, as a pure gift, the one called Jesus, who is above the stars and at the same time has "pitched his tent among us." How fortunate and utterly privileged we would be to come to see and know this Jesus in our life.

• • •

## PERSONAL REFLECTION

*Spend at least twenty minutes thinking about the humanity of God in Jesus and everything that he experienced on earth. How does this reality affect your view of and relationship to God? Does it make it easier to approach God?*

# UNFAILING LOVE

*"God Is Love."*

*~1 John 4:16*

WHEN WE CONSIDER THE VASTNESS OF THE universe and the extraordinary wonder, majesty, and power that would need to reside within the God who created it all, how could we not fear? However in Christian revelation there is another dimension to consider, one more wonderful than the cosmos itself: The one who created it all loves us.

From the perspective of Christian faith it is all about love. The problem is that we think we have heard all of this before. The response many people have to "God is love" often goes something like this: "Yeah, I heard that already. I know God loves me. That is nice. I guess when I die and there is a heaven, we will all go there because this God loves us. I guess that is what it is all about."

I believe that we respond this way because we have not

put forth the effort or have not had the humility to really *listen* to what the ramifications are from the statement "God is love." Have we truly pondered, with effort and humility, what a God who loves us means?

The revelation is this: "God is love." (1 John 4:16) This is a true "revelation," since throughout human history "God as love" was not to be found. Gods were almost always capricious, demanding, vengeful, and requiring appeasement—just think of virtually any story involving the ancient Greek gods. No one knew completely where he/she stood with God: it was all very precarious. If there is a God then it is very possible that God made things for enjoyment, to play with. It would be equally possible that God does *not*, in fact, love us. This would make the fact that we exist at all not necessarily "good news," but rather almost certainly "bad news." In other words, if God isn't love and God is the creator of the universe, we would be in trouble and our lives would be a rather sick joke. Imagine living life, conscious or unconscious before a God who cares about nothing but his own enjoyment. Knowing the greatness of the universe would only leave us cowering in dark corners before an immensely powerful God. On the other hand, we might simply stay blissfully unaware until the awe-filled or "awful" day when we meet God.

Something new came into history and the consciousness of humanity, however, with the coming of Jesus of Nazareth: a singular God whose very nature is Love. The Creator God of this universe *loves* us. This may not sound like much at first (because we have heard it so many times before), but this may be the most startling good news of all. If "God is love" is true, then what kind of love is this, and what kind of meaning does our existence have? It is very hard to begin to grasp the meaning of the word love since it, like faith, has undergone a significant dumbing down. Love in our culture has almost exclusively been reduced to emotion and sensuality. We consider love to be real when we "feel" it. The word love is even used to manipulate our emotions and sell products. I remember when I was growing up in New York, I saw an advertising promotion for a beer that said, "Only love is better than Schlitz." Even as a young person I could see something wrong with this. I thought to myself, *Well, this beer must be quite amazing* (and I knew no beer could be that good) *or love is not much of a big deal after all.*

I remember a time when my notion of "God is Love" was stretched to a new understanding.

I grew up in New York in the sixties and we played many sports during my childhood except one—soccer. I never played soccer and when I watched it on television I found it to be very boring. *What are all these Europeans getting all excited about?* I thought to myself. In my mind this was the most uninteresting of sports.

Many years later my oldest son came of age to play a team sport. Times had certainly changed and now everyone was playing soccer. Naturally he joined a soccer team as well, and I can still remember his first game and my reaction. On the way to the game I was feeling sorry for myself, thinking, *Oh great, now I have to watch soccer on a Saturday afternoon and pretend it is really interesting. The things I do for my children. How soon will it be over?* I forced a smile and an excited look at my son as he ran onto the soccer field when the game began. What happened next was quite unexpected and startling. After watching the game for a few minutes I became transfixed. I watched with great intensity and, even more shocking, I started to get involved and actually care. I began to shout, softly at first but later loudly, words of encouragement and even direction. "Come on, you can do it. Faster, faster. Oh look, he is open, pass the ball, pass the ball. Shoot...shoot!" Before I knew it I was running up and down the side of the field shouting, cheering, directing, and even complaining at the calls of the referee against our team. Here I was, looking like a madman, telling people what to do even though I didn't know anything.

After the game I thought to myself, *What just happened? What came over me? Why did I act that way?* Then I realized what was different here: My son was in the game. That alone is what made all the difference. I then thought that if I would react like this because of my love for my son, with all my limitations, how does God react, with God's perfect love, when we are in the game of life and in the game of faith? This small human interaction between my son and me is one of the many ways I have been stretched to a new understanding of what it means to say "God loves us." In the human encounters of our lives we are often invited to a revelation of God's love for us. This encounter with my son was no exception. It held for me a new and startling insight into God's Love. I began to see how mighty that love of God must be, how "on our side." How God must cheer for us, pull for us, think about us, yearn for us. Especially during times of crisis and struggle, how God wants the very best for us. One of the classical definitions of love is "to will what is good for the other." In the Christian faith we even believe that Jesus intercedes for us, prays for us, all the time, at every moment of our lives. What a mighty prayer that must be. If God loves us much more than I love my son, without limitation, then what a powerful, cosmic love that must be. A love capable of filling the universe is capable of filling each moment of our lives and filling it with a presence so dynamic and positive it would change the game of life and faith completely.

One of the greatest Christian thinkers of all time is Thomas Aquinas. He said, "To love is to will another's existence." That means that if there is a God who is love, and if that love fills the universe, then that love, by its very nature, wills our existence, at each moment of our lives, even at this very moment. The fact that we exist means that we are loved. Right now, right here.

St. Augustine said, "It is because God is good that we are, that we exist." That means that we were not created out of necessity; God did not need us. We were not created out of justice; God owed us nothing. No, it is to God's sheer love that we owe our existence.

If this is true then there must have been a cosmic dance of joy the day each of us were born—a cosmic dance of the God who loves us and delights in us at every moment of our existence. What a dance that must be! Our very existence gives God joy. To live within this God, our fears would subside and be replaced by joy.

·  ·  ·

## PERSONAL REFLECTION

*Think of God as "on your side," pulling for you, cheering for you, wanting what is best for you. How does this affect or change your notion of God? How does this make you feel?*

# FALLING IN LOVE WITH GOD

*"Wasn't it like a fire burning within us."*
*~Luke 24:32*

G OD'S LOVE BECOMES REAL FOR US WHEN
we become "real" to it, when we open up the truth of
who we are, in this present moment in which we live.
Speaking to God from our hearts, from the intimacy of our soul,
opening to God our deepest longings, fears, desires, hopes, and
dreams. Then we would have the disposition to come to really
"know" God with a new intimacy in our lives. This "knowing" of
God's love is not simply a rational knowing or assent or agreement
to a religious truth. On the contrary, this knowing is more of the
kind in the Hebrew Scriptures that speaks how Abraham "knew"
Sarah. Abraham not only knew Sarah rationally, but also emotionally,
physically, sexually—with intuitive and spiritual knowledge.
"Knowing" like this is the complete way one who loves another

comes to know the other. Couples who have been married for years come to know each other in this way—they know what the other is thinking before it is said, they know what the other will think before a question is asked. This is how we are invited to "know" the love that surrounds us—to experience it, to know this love in all the ways and dimensions that a human can know.

"I know my wife loves me." It is reasonable for me to say this since anyone can observe how she acts toward me. At the same time I cannot prove this to another person. I have come to know this throughout a life that is shared intimately together, revealed in countless acts, encounters, and experiences of the other in our shared life. Love is something that gradually grows in its depths and understanding in order that it may become real to us, and once real this love becomes something we believe in with all our hearts and can count on in so many ways.

Even though love develops gradually, it can also surprise us with a spontaneous depth that is life-changing as well. When two people fall in love, it is a transformative experience. We may have known the other for some time, but one day the other stands out from the crowd. It is as if everyone else on this earth fades out of focus while this one other stands out in radiant clarity and light. Our minds can think of no one else and our heart beats in a new way only for this one person. Even our everyday lives change. I remember noticing my daughter in her first year of marriage doing the dishes in her apartment. In the twenty-five years of her life before her marriage, she had never once cleaned a dish unless she was asked—but that has certainly changed. Now my daughter does her own and her husband's dishes every day, and she does them willingly and happily. Love changes us, even our most stubborn habits.

The energy and joy we discover when we love is very real. This same "falling in love" that happens between human beings happens as well between a human and the Divine. In other words, it is possible for us to "fall in love" with God and discover a romance with divine love that is like no other we have known. Not only is it possible, but in some form this must happen. Much like how two people fall in love with each other over time, we "fall in love" with God over time and after a lifetime of experiences. Countless people throughout the ages have spoken of their falling in love with the God who loves them, singing of the divine romance they have discovered. Augustine affirms this as well: "To fall in love with God is the greatest of all romances; to seek Him, the greatest adventure; to find Him, the greatest human achievement." This love is also passionately expressed in the Hebrew Scriptures in the Song of Solomon (also known as the Song of Songs):

*Let him kiss me with the kisses of his mouth! For*
*your love is better than wine, your name is perfume*
*poured out.... The king has brought me into his*
*chambers. We will exult and rejoice in you; we will*
*extol your love more than wine; rightly do they*
*love you.... Set me as a seal upon your heart, as*
*a seal upon your arm; for love is strong as death,*
*passion fierce as the grave. Its flashes are flashes of*
*fire, a raging flame. Many waters cannot quench*
*love, neither can floods drown it. (1:2-4; 8:-7)*

There is nothing dull in the experience of divine love. Dullness, not doubt, is the strongest enemy of faith. Faith comes from a disposition of the heart, from imagination, from the humility of listening, from the readiness to learn something not known before, from the childlike freedom of letting go and receiving that which is new. Our ability to discover faith is in direct proportion to the amount of truth and wonder we can take in without running away. Dullness enters our lives when we allow ourselves to be distracted from the love and wonder that surround us. It is like the lion tamer who enters the cage carrying only a chair and a whip, knowing that the key to taming the lion is to distract him. By placing objects in the lion's face to distract his gaze, and by cracking a whip to distract the lion with noise, the lion tamer can control the most ferocious of beasts, making it jump through silly little hoops. In the same way, distraction can tame us into believing in and living for silly things and jumping through other people's hoops.

I am reminded of a car commercial I recently saw that depicts a family driving through the country in a very nice SUV. Throughout the commercial, the camera focuses on the beauty that surrounds the car as it drives through a lush countryside filled with colors, light, and wonder. At the end of the advertisement, we see the parents smiling at one another right before the camera pans over the children in the backseat, watching a cartoon on the car's television screen. The children are completely distracted and oblivious to all that is surrounding them. This commercial is just one of the many reminders of how often we can pass through life—distracted, oblivious, not seeing all that surrounds us at every moment of our existence, never considering what it might be saying. It's rather like working with someone for several years, sharing only limited experiences with them and never really taking the time to get to know them. Sometimes, though, we get the opportunity to spend time with that person outside of work, at a mutual friend's party or some other event where we find ourselves in a deep conversation, and then our eyes are opened to the beauty within that person. He/she was there all the while but we did not really know them, and now a friendship and a type of love is possible that was not before.

When we look at the sands of the seashore, or examine an individual snowflake, we come to realize that in all the sands in all the deserts and seashores and in all the snows that ever fell to this earth, no two grains of sand, no two snowflakes, are alike. Consider that each of us has a retina and a fingerprint like no one else in this world, that there is no one who thinks the way I do, dreams the way I do, laughs the way I do, cries the way I do. We are all made in the image and likeness of God, and that we reflect something unique of the Divine that no one else on this planet does or ever will have, gives each of us a radically new possibility in how we see ourselves and one another. We are not infinitesimal forms of life clinging to cosmic dust. No, we are the Creator's creation, made with an ability to know God and to "know" Divine Love. We are here, we exist, and that very existence is a statement of God's love.

Ralph Waldo Emerson said, "All I have seen teaches me to trust the Creator for all I have not seen." How absolutely wonderful it must be, what awaits us. For "what no eye has seen, nor ear heard, nor the human heart conceived, what God has prepared for those who love him" (1 Corinthians 2:9). More amazing than the wonders of the universe is the revelation of the God who loves us, each one of us uniquely, at every moment.

This revelation of divine love even takes a further step, astounding us with a God of the cosmos for whom, "even the hairs of your head are all counted" (Matthew 10:30). A cosmic

God that fills the universe and, at the same time, is so personal, so intimate, that this God has numbered the hairs on our head and knows each of us personally. A God who knows why we do what we do, and fail to do what we want to do; who knows all our inner contradictions and conflicts, the things which afflict us and that which has wounded us. God knows it all—and still loves us. This God is always attentive to us, always thinks about us, always yearns for the best for us, always roots for us, smiles upon us, and longs for us to succeed in this journey of life—because that is what love does. This is the one who leads us "with cords of human kindness, with bands of love" (Hosea 11:4). This is the God of the Universe.

In the book of Isaiah, the northern kingdom was invaded and Jerusalem was under attack. During this time of crisis, the people wondered if God had forgotten them. Isaiah wrote to them: "Can a woman forget her nursing child, or show no compassion for the child of her womb? Even these may forget, yet I will never forget you. See, I have inscribed you on the palms of my hands" (49:15-6). The God of the Hebrew Scriptures loves like the God of the Christian Scriptures whose hand was indeed carved with a nail for love of us all. These wounds are taken with the risen Jesus into glory. They are always with him because our wounds are His wounds, because He is love.

Often in life there are times when we feel under attack, wounded, and may wonder if God has indeed forgotten us. In reality, we are particularly loved at those times, much like a parent's love is heightened when a child suffers. It is especially during these times that the God who is pulling for us and rooting for us is most moved by our condition. It is in the very midst of crisis, uncertainty, and struggle that divine love is most present to us, inviting us to know and experience this God of love, the one who holds you in the palm of His hand.

· · ·

## PERSONAL REFLECTION

*How has your relationship with God developed over your lifetime? Have you fallen in love with God yet?*

# The Church
# of the Second
# Chance

*"I must stay at your house today."*
*~Luke 19:5*

I T IS REMARKABLE TO IMAGINE THE GOD OF THE
Universe as a fetus in his mother's womb, totally dependent on
his parents. When the time of Jesus' birth arrived, his parents
were traveling down a long road. A young, homeless couple, they
were dealing with a pregnancy that was suspect by all who knew
them. Birth was imminent and the young couple was becoming
increasingly anxious, looking for a place where their child could
be born. They knocked on the doors of strangers, asking for help,
and over and over again they were given the same answer: "No."
There was no room for them.

To imagine the God of this cosmos, dependent and asking for
help and getting rejected, is quite alarming. I often wonder about
the innkeepers who turned away the Son of God and his parents.

If there is an eternity, do they spend it looking back on that missed opportunity, wondering how different life would have been if they had welcomed in that young, pregnant couple? When God came asking for help, knocking on doors, they said, "No. There is no room. We are too busy." They could have received and given aid to the God of all creation, but they said no.

This says something about our human condition and our relationship with the Divine: It is not good. It doesn't take much reading or exposure to human history and world events to know that something is wrong with our human family. This becomes apparent when we ask the questions, "Why is humanity this way? Why is the world this way? Why am I this way? Why am I filled with so many contradictions? Why am I stuck in things I do not like and do not want?"

Perhaps I wonder about those innkeepers because I once found myself with a similar choice.

• • •

Every Christmas Eve, my family sits down for a special dinner in our family room with a roaring fire in the hearth. Every year, the food, the decorations, the company are all very nice. This feast is a special time just for my wife, myself, and our three children, and it's a celebration that we look forward to each Christmas.

One year when my daughter was in high school, she had a

friend whose family was going through some tough times. Even though they lived in the same house, they would not be celebrating Christmas together. My daughter mentioned to me that her friend wanted to come over to give her a gift on Christmas Eve. I replied, "That's fine, as long as it's not during our family time tonight." Sure enough, the doorbell rang during the dinner. I looked through the window and saw my daughter's friend at the door.

I started to protest, but my daughter interrupted me: "I told her, Dad. I don't know why she came now."

Annoyed, I replied, "Let her in, go in the living room, and make it quick." She did what I asked and once her friend left, we returned to our dinner.

Several months later, I read the passage in the New Testament where Mary and Joseph are going door to door, looking for a place where Jesus could be born. In a moment of clarity, I realized that Jesus had come to me as well on Christmas Eve, the night we celebrate his birth, looking for a place to be born. He had come in the form of that young woman, a woman whose family was struggling through a bad time and who may have wanted nothing more than a warm and comforting place where she was welcome. She literally knocked at my door. And I said no.

In Matthew 25:40, Jesus makes it clear that how we receive the outcasts, the poor, and those in need is how we receive him. When I think about myself at that moment on Christmas Eve, I do not like what I see. I am ashamed. My actions that night are indicative of other ways that I continue to say "no" even though I profess to be one who says "yes." Of course, in some ways I was right in my feelings of wanting to have a special evening with my family, but we can be wrong in our rightness. Love is not about being "right." I was wrong that night. I didn't say "hello" to this young woman, or even "Merry Christmas." I was deeply wrong.

About four years later, it was Christmas Eve once again, and the same dinner was prepared and served in the same family room before the same fireplace. During dinner there was a knock at the door. When I opened it, I saw a young man, pale and shaking, standing before me. The man explained that he had lost control of his car on the ice and ran into a car parked on our street. Seeing the lights on in our windows, he came to our house to ask for help. We quickly brought him in and my wife, who is a nurse practitioner, checked him for injuries. We gave him something warm to drink, comforted him, settled him down, checked his car, and called his parents. I had to smile as my daughter oh-so-generously proceeded to console him with tales of all five of our children's car accidents. As she recounted each incident, the young man became increasingly encouraged, growing calm in light of his circumstances. (Compared to stories about our family, his accident was really quite minor.) In the end, it turned out to be a wonderful night. Once the young man left, we all returned to our dinner, energized by the time we had spent helping him.

Several months later I read the same passage of Mary and Joseph looking for a place for Jesus to be born. I remembered the past Christmas Eve, and I realized once again that Jesus had come to me, literally knocking on my door...and this time I said "yes." I understood in that moment I had been given a second chance to say yes to God. I was deeply moved within, not because I said yes, but by the offer of a second chance—the offer of mercy.

We are all given second chances, and third and fourth and fifth chances as well. The wonderful news is that God has given all of humanity the ultimate second chance through the life and death of Jesus Christ. We have all said "no" to God at one point or another—and throughout our lives, we will continue to say "no" in our brokenness far too often—but we are all given the gift of a second chance, a chance to say "yes." The life of Jesus among us is God's way of giving all of us a second chance. When we come together in this belief in Jesus, we are essentially coming together as the Church of the Second Chance. And everyone is welcome to the Church of the Second Chance.

The group that best exemplifies this way of welcoming is Alcoholics Anonymous. In AA meetings, members always begin by introducing themselves. It goes like this...

*"My name is Jerry, and I am an alcoholic."*

The group replies, "Hi, Jerry. Welcome."

If we who believe in and follow Jesus could gather like this, in courage and humility, perhaps we could each stand up in faith and speak the truth to one another. Perhaps it would go something like this...

*"My name is Susan, and I am very judgmental of others."*

"Hi, Susan. Welcome."

*"My name is Peter. I stab people in the back to get ahead at work."*

"Hi, Peter. Welcome."

*"My name is Margaret. I have many hurt feelings, and I am filled with bitterness."*

"Hi, Margaret. Welcome."

*"My name is Tony, and I live for myself. I ignore the needy and the poor. I do nothing about social injustice."*

"Hi, Tony. Welcome."

*"My name is Joan, and I am a gossip.*

"Hi, Joan. Welcome."

*"My name is Bill. I am addicted to pornography."*

"Hi, Bill. Welcome."

*"My name is Veronica, and I am unfaithful to my spouse."*

"Hi, Veronica. Welcome."

*"My name is Matt, and I am a liar."*

"Hi, Matt. Welcome."

*"My name is Jack. I live for money, and I am greedy."*

"Hi, Jack. Welcome."

*"My name is Sandra, and I am religious—I go to church, but I have never surrendered anything to God because I am too afraid."*

"Hi, Sandra. Welcome."

*"My name is Michelle, and I am angry with God and angry at the church."*

"Hi, Michelle. Welcome."

*"My name is Tom, and this is my first time at church...I am not sure what I believe."*

"Hi, Tom. Welcome."

We are all welcome. When we recognize this, we can turn to one another and offer the same welcome that Jesus Christ offers us. Teresa of Avila was known to pray for the salvation of Judas. People would ask her, "Why would you do that? Judas betrayed Jesus!" Unflinching, she would reply, "So did I." We have all fallen short, we have all said "no" to God—and we are all given a second chance to say "yes." With God, there is always another chance. And if we recognize this and live within its reality, then nothing can keep us from God's love. And that is good news, indeed.

• • •

## PERSONAL REFLECTION

*What does thinking about Christianity as the*
*"Church of the Second Chance" mean to you?*

# MERCY

*"While he was still far off..."*
*~Luke 15:20*

E XAMINING THE LIFE OF JESUS REVEALS THE very nature of divine love present within him, and we find that Jesus' life was nearly 100% focused on those who had strayed away from God, those who were not connected to or even looking for God, and those who lived as if life had little or nothing to do with divine reality. Jesus did not preach to those who were already convinced of their salvation. Instead he ministered to those furthest from religion.

In Jesus we discover that God is moved to act mercifully. Relying on story to illustrate his point, Jesus relates how God constantly strives to bring home those who have become distant from God. He tells the story of the shepherd who, having lost one sheep in the wilderness, leaves his flock of ninety-nine sheep in search of the one who is lost, just as "there will be more joy in heaven over one sinner who repents than over ninety-nine righteous persons who need no repentance" (Luke 15:7). A story like this really does not make logical sense. After all, why sacrifice the good of the many for the safety of the one?

If this were not enough, Jesus tells one of the most popular and enduring parables from the New Testament: the return of the prodigal son. In it we find an unloving, spoiled child who asks for his share of his father's estate. In Jesus' times, that would be like saying to one's father, "You are dead to me." Under Jewish law, a father could have responded any way he chose to a son who made such a request, even going so far as to order his son put to death. But in Jesus' story, the father honors his son's request, giving him his entire share of the estate. And from then on, the father waits night and day for his son to return, searching the horizon in hope that he will see his son return home.

Indeed, the day finally comes when the son returns after squandering all the money and living sinfully, and the father catches a glimpse of him in the distance. Jesus tells us that "while he [the son] was still far off, his father saw him and was filled with compassion" (Luke 15:20). Though he had every reason to feel nothing but anger and resentment, the father rejoiced at his son's return, running out to greet his son, clothing him, and embracing him, all the while ignoring the son's protestation: "I am no longer worthy to be called your son." (Luke 15:21) Immediately, the father calls for a celebration and spends even more of his wealth on what most of us would view as an ungrateful, wretched child.

No one lives life this way. It just is not how things are done, and we all know that. When we have been wronged, we wait for the offender to make a complete apology, then wait some more to see that the apology is genuine, then we wait even longer to see that the offender has really changed his/her behavior. That process makes sense to us. And once we finally accept the one who has hurt us, our acceptance is rarely more than conditional and partial, for we keep our distance until he/she is able to prove his/her character to our satisfaction.

It may be an extraordinarily difficult thing to understand and to believe, but the God revealed in Jesus Christ does not relate to offense the way that we do, for God shows a mercy that transcends all understanding and all reason. To us, Jesus' story of the prodigal son may make little sense. In fact, many of us may quietly accuse Jesus of being weak or soft. Yet it is only when we come to know this mercy and experience it ourselves that all the words and actions and stories of Jesus begin to make sense. For divine love has a logic which our reason does not understand, and there is a reasonableness to love that is not reasonable without it. If we look at the life of Jesus without looking through the lens of love, and if we choose to examine his life the same way we might examine someone's in our world, much of Jesus' ministry will appear to be quite silly. But once we look at the Gospel through the eyes of love, a love that is mercy itself, we see that Jesus' life, his ministry, and his message make more than good sense; they begin to look irresistible. How good it is that God's ways are not our ways "For my thoughts are not your thoughts, nor are your ways my ways, says the Lord. For as the heavens are higher than the earth, so are my ways higher than your ways and my thoughts than your thoughts." Isaiah 55:8-9

The actions and passions of Jesus reveal that having mercy for those who are "still far off" was a central concern of his while he was on this earth. Jesus' whole focus and the very purpose of his life was centered upon those who have lost their way. He moved from village to village, searching out those who needed to be found, in order to proclaim the good news of God's mercy and forgiveness. Along the way we find Jesus saying: "Those who are well have no need of a physician, but those who are sick; I have come to call not the righteous but sinners" (Mark 2:17). "How often have I desired to gather your children together as a hen gathers her brood under her wings" (Luke 13:34). "Your sins are forgiven you" (Luke 5:20). He was often found eating with sinners and tax collectors, and this very act was a profound public statement of Jesus' acceptance of his dining partners. Even as he was taking his last breath, Jesus extended mercy to one more person, the thief who died alongside him.

Jesus' life shows us the nature of the "love" that he revealed: mercy. It is all mercy. Mercy is ever-present and for all, with no exception. It is freely given. Mercy loves at the precise moment when one is most undeserving. Mercy does not wait for us. It seeks. Mercy is stirred to action because the one lost does not know he/she is in need of it.

Augustine is one who met this mercy in his life and he writes eloquently about the experience:

"You have called to me, cried out, and you broke through my deafness. You have flashed forth with light, and have shone upon me, and have put my blindness to flight! You breathed your fragrance on me; I drew in breath and now I pant for you. I have tasted you, now I hunger and thirst for more. You have touched me, and I have burned for your peace."

When we experience the "flash," the "taste" of mercy, it becomes irresistible. When the light goes on that this mercy has been with us all along the way of our lives, everything is seen in this new light.

One of my favorite memories of my children growing up is the manner in which they would often greet me when I came home from work. I would walk in the door and they would exclaim, "Dad's home!" They would scamper towards me from different parts of the house, emitting an indistinguishable sound of childhood glee as they came, and then proceed to jump and grab on to some part of my body, dragging me to the floor. Once on the carpet they would laugh as I tickled them and held them close. Sometimes we would play "horsey" and I would let them ride on my back as I carried them around the room on all fours "One more time, Dad!" they would squeal, and of course they received another turn. It was a very special moment, repeated day after day without tiring, each as wonderful as the last. Then a strange thing happened. They changed.

One day a teenager emerged. Something took over my children. I would begin to get strange blank stares when I talked to them. They looked right at me, but they didn't see me. *Where were they?* I would wonder. *Where did they go? Did aliens take them?* I would come home and there would be nothing, just silence. Coming in the door and yelling, "Hello! Hello? I'm home...?" Silence.

Occasionally I would get a voice from upstairs yelling back, "Yo, Dad."

"'Yo, Dad'?" I would mutter to myself. "Incredible."

This went on for years, and eventually the aliens returned my children as I noticed another change that began to occur. My daughter went away to college, met a variety of people, and traveled to many places abroad. My son went to a large public high school where he, too, met a large cross-section of people with many different family experiences. I remember one day I came home and my son asked to talk to me. He had a serious question he was dealing with, and he really listened to what I said. Afterwards, he thanked me and put his arm around my shoulder. Another day I came home and out of nowhere my daughter ran up and threw her arms around me. How very sweet those moments were, and perhaps even sweeter than when they were children, because now they *chose* me, freely, as adults.

You see, they changed, but I had not. My love for them was always the same. It was always in their midst, waiting, looking, but they didn't always recognize it. So it is with the God that Jesus brings to us, the One whom he calls "Father." This is the divine love we are called to ponder and consider for ourselves no matter what place we find ourselves in life. This is the startling good news of God's mercy that is present and revealed even in the most challenging and confusing times in our lives, the times when we are most in need.

In the movie *A Man for All Seasons*, Thomas More is in prison for defying the king and following his Christian conscience. His daughter is beseeching him to change his position, and she keeps saying to him that he must be reasonable, that what he is doing does not make sense. His last reply to her pleading is this: "Finally, it is not a matter of reason, it is a matter of love." More must do what he must do, not because it is reasonable but because it is the loving thing to do. And so it is for us: not a matter of what is reasonable, but a matter of love—the divine love that is Mercy, always present, always offered, waiting and looking out over the horizon in our direction, even though we may still be far off.

God's merciful love is without limits. "Equal to his majesty is his mercy." (Sirach 2:18). This great, cosmic, marvelous God is *all mercy*. The greatness of the cosmos is equaled by only one thing: mercy. In this light, every single one of our offenses is like a drop of water thrown into a flaming furnace of infinite love and acceptance and renewal.

After hearing all this we may respond by saying, "This is just too good to be true. There has to be some catch." Our only answer is that the God of the Cosmos who came as one of us, lived among us, and even died on a cross, is the only one who can give a gift this beautiful, this good.

I know of no one who says this more beautifully than Jean d'Elbee in his reflections on the mercy of God as understood by Therese of Liseaux:

> *And that moves us, overwhelms us. If we come to*
> *the point of comprehending that we are loved to a*
> *supreme, unimaginable degree, unto silent, gratuitous,*
> *cruel death, to the point of total immolation by*
> *Him whom we do not even know, or if we have*
> *known Him, whom we have denied and offended;*
> *if we come to the point of comprehending that we*
> *are the objects of such a love, of so great a love, we*
> *cannot remain complacent.* (I Believe in Love)

Why are we here? Why were we born? Because God has chosen us to receive this love. God's mercy is out there, waiting, looking out over the horizon in our direction, anxious for us to return home just as we are.

. . .

## PERSONAL REFLECTION

*How does God's pure and unending mercy*
*affect the way you see yourself and live?*

# THE CRUCIFIED GOD

*"They crucified Jesus there with the criminals,*
*one on his right and one on his left."*
*~Luke 23:33*

I T IS VERY DIFFICULT FOR US WHO HAVE
inherited 2,000 years of Christian history to have any notion
of just how scandalous and utterly abhorrent it was that
Jesus was executed on a cross. We live in a world where the cross
is a piece of jewelry. All sorts of people wear a cross: working
professionals, rock stars, small children, grandparents. Often made
of gold or silver (though occasionally studded with diamonds),
crosses today are more of a fashion statement than a statement
of faith. But if we look back in time, we see a startlingly different
view of the cross.

In the ancient Roman world, crucifixion was reserved for
slaves, pirates, or enemies of the state. It often occurred in a
public place and passersby would ridicule and mock those hanging

from the crucifix. Roman citizens were generally exempt from crucifixion, and it was used primarily as a means to humiliate and disgrace the condemned.

When Jesus indicated to his disciples that he would suffer and die, Peter took Jesus aside and scolded him like a parent does to a child, outraged he would even suggest such a thing. At Jesus' death all of his followers (except a few women from a distance) left Jesus alone. The most ancient versions of Mark's gospel, the earliest written gospel, ended with the fear and distress of the women present, as Mark depicts for us the utter confusion and terror that the news of Jesus' death on the cross evoked in his dejected, disoriented disciples. So stunned were they by the event, they were afraid to tell anyone what had happened.

It is fascinating to note that Jesus' crucifixion was so difficult for the early Christians that right from the beginning they were unable to depict the crucifixion in any form of Christian art. The first crucifixion scene is carved in wood on a side door of the Basilica of Santa Sabina, a fifth century Roman church. In other words, it took the early Christians four hundred years to bring themselves to portray the crucifixion of their Messiah. The historian Thomas Cahill comments on this directly in his book Desire of the Everlasting Hills:

*The central fact of Jesus' life, his grisly suffering and death, so traumatized the first Christians and even though it was a central reality to contend with, they could not bear to look at it directly. Only in the fifth century, nearly a century after they discontinued the practice of crucifixion and no one living had witnessed such a procedure, did Christians forget the shame and horror of the event sufficiently to begin to make pictures of it.*

The death of Jesus meant that a people accustomed to shedding the blood of animals (and sometimes people) for God had to contend with the revelation of a God who shed his blood for them. This was simply too much; it turned everything upside down. The first century Christian writer Tertullian put it more bluntly, "God's son died: it is believable precisely because it is absurd. He was buried and rose again: it is certain because it is impossible."

So what about us, 2,000 years later, so comfortable with the image of Jesus of Nazareth dying upon a cross? What if instead of a cross, we saw an electric chair with straps to hold down the arms, torso, and legs, and the cap and sponge to cover the head and allow the electric current to pass through it? What if we saw the cross in and of itself as the ultimate statement of weakness, failure, rejection, suffering, and agonizing death? That is what the people at the time of Jesus saw. How comfortable would we be as well, if we saw the cross for what it *really* was?

How easy is it to think about "a crucified God?" How comfortable are we with a cross that shows the weakness of God, the failure of God, the suffering of God? The cross is not meant to be an image of comfort, but an image of *hope*. We can see in the cross of Jesus something unexpected, a God who is weak with us who are weak, a God who is a failure with us who fail, a God who suffers with us who suffer—a God who dies with us who die.

## THE WEAKNESS OF GOD

The scandal of Jesus is not only that he came as one of us but also in the manner in which he came. He was born in the midst of animals. His father had to protect him from those who sought to kill him. Imagine the God of the Universe needing help from a human to be born and needing someone to protect him from other humans whom he created. And if that was not enough, he "was crucified in weakness." (2 Corinthians 13:4) The God who has the power to create the cosmos exposed weakness and vulnerability before us all. What kind of message does that give us? I believe the fear of being weak drives many of us, and the cross is our invitation to let go of our fear.

Hidden within this reality is an invitation to welcome weakness and vulnerability into our lives. We are free to be weak, to be vulnerable, because God was so weak and vulnerable to us. This is hard for us to understand. I remember my last day of working with a group of young people in a church one summer. Early in the day, someone approached me and said, "Thank you, John, for all you did this summer. I really appreciated your efforts and found you to be a very fine person, but I have to say I don't think I really ever got to know you."

Of course, being such an open person, my first reaction was to think to myself, *Well, that's his problem.* Later that same day another person came to me and said essentially the same thing. It was that evening after a third person (all unbeknownst to one another) shared with me the same thoughts. By that point I had gotten the message. I was a nice guy: I helped others, people liked me, but I did not allow anyone to get close to me. I was in control and I was afraid of being vulnerable to others. Nice things happened in my interactions, but intimacy and real community did not.

Another time, I was going through a period when I was particularly critical of religious people, especially those who were priests, pastors, and in religious communities. One day, I attended a talk by a famous preacher who was also a Franciscan. Knowing he would be wearing his Franciscan robes, I said to myself, *I'll check out his shoes, and if they are expensive I will know he sold out and is not a true Franciscan* (Franciscans commit themselves to lifelong poverty). Just as I was thinking these thoughts, the Franciscan came out to speak, and I immediately noticed that he only had socks on his feet. He wasn't even wearing shoes, let alone expensive ones. I was stunned. I thought to myself, *I could never do that in front of so many people.* (Later he mentioned that he had bought new shoes but they hurt his feet, so he was just wearing his socks.) I didn't hear a word of his talk, because in that moment I heard what I needed to hear: I heard about myself and my true weaknesses, my rush to judgment, my negativity, my fault-finding. I heard my insecurity.

How freeing it is to admit the truth about ourselves, whatever it may be, and to let it go. For only the truth will really set us free. "I am a bitter person, I am negative, jealous, greedy. I am filled with self pity." Why not admit it? To allow ourselves to be weak enough to see the truth of who we are is so very liberating. The cross of Jesus gives us that permission. If God in Jesus can be weak, we most certainly can be as well, for once we acknowledge our weakness, we open ourselves to spiritual insight, freedom, and true strength.

I will never forget a talk I heard from a Catholic priest who shared his own personal experience about coming to terms with weakness. For several years, the priest said daily Mass at his church for a small group made up mostly of older women. One day a member of that group came to him and mentioned that the woman who always sat in the first pew recently died. At that moment he realized that he didn't even know her name...and more importantly he realized he didn't even care to know her. During his talk, the priest said, "I saw the depths of my own hypocrisy." I had never heard anyone speak that openly—never, much less a religious person. I knew I could allow myself to be weak in the company of a person like that. I could confess my truths to him, because he had just confessed his to me. After hearing him speak, I was free to see and recognize my own hypocrisy by having the opportunity to see and recognize his.

To bring our weakness into the light of day, without fear, is not only very liberating. It is a disposition required for us to meet the God of Weakness. It is here in our genuine state of imperfection that our weakness is transformed and, in a strange way, it becomes our strength. Many times I have known people who, for whatever reason, I found to be difficult to associate with. They rubbed me the wrong way and I had trouble mustering the patience to deal with them. Then one day they would come and talk with me and open up about their lives. I would see for the first time what was really going on inside of them. I would see what they carried, what was unresolved in their lives, how hard it was for them to be who they were and live their lives. Immediately this would change not only my perception of them but even how I interacted with them. I found it so much easier to love them and be patient, to be understanding and compassionate. I know now what a gift it is each time someone exposes their weaknesses and vulnerabilities to me, for they are risking much. I have never met a person whom I have really come to know that I could not love.

Might it be the same with God? We cannot know the depths of God's love until we expose our own weaknesses.

This makes no sense unless we really hear Jesus' words: Do not be afraid. We do not need to be afraid in the presence of Jesus, for he came without power, putting it all aside, so that we would be able to approach him. What if Jesus came, not in weakness, but in the power of God? That would be quite a show. All of humanity would cower in fear before such a sight, do whatever we were told, and "believe" what he said to believe. But God in Jesus chose another way: the way of weakness. God knows that to love another, it cannot be because we fear them, for that is not real love. We must come to God without fear, for love and fear cannot coexist. "Perfect love casts out fear." 1 John 4:18

Perhaps this explains that the ones who received Jesus and welcomed him into their hearts and lives when he was on the earth were indeed the weak ones, not the religious and powerful class—they missed him. Who was at the birth of Jesus? Mary and Joseph: two poor individuals from an oppressed class, dealing with a questionable pregnancy and temporary homelessness. Then there were the shepherds, who at that time were the poorest of the poor, living with animals and away from society, unclean outcasts who were suspect to all and who did not go to church. Mary, Joseph, and the shepherds—it was to them that the Good News was first proclaimed. They were the first to see God in human form. That is quite a message for those of us who may have recently lost a job or much of our savings, quite a message for someone who may be feeling like a failure. In light of this gospel, we are all in good company. We are in a very good place, the very place in which Jesus is born—not in a stable, but in the intimacy of the human soul.

How can any one of us think we are not included in God's great Heart of Love? It is those who recognize their weaknesses that are the ones most receptive to accepting God into their lives. In our weakness we are most free to receive the one who became weak for us. There is finally one with whom we can let it all go. We can come just as we are. We do not have to pretend to be someone we are not. What good news that is.

. . .

## PERSONAL REFLECTION

*Think of the ways in which you are afraid to let your weaknesses show. Have there been times when you exposed your weaknesses to another person? If you have, do you think it helped you? If not, what has been stopping you?*

# THE FAILURE
# OF GOD

*"But we had hoped that he was the one to redeem Israel."*
*~Luke 24:21*

"**I**T COULD NOT HAVE ENDED IN A WORSE WAY. Jesus on the cross is a total and abject failure."

This is what the cross communicated to all who looked upon it, and why all of Jesus' followers ran away. And then Jesus lay in the tomb for three days before his reported resurrection. Why let everything sit in failure? What kind of statement did God in Jesus make by lying in the darkness of failure and death? Jesus Christ embraced that which we fear the most—failure. In doing so he shared with us the grace that gives us permission and freedom to accept our own failures—the very things we run away from—and in those most surprising of places, meet him there.

The thought of failure stirs up interesting things inside us, doesn't it? I remember recently seeing a T-shirt that read, "Second place is the first loser." *What a way to go through life*, I thought when I saw it. I know a woman who at one point couldn't say she was divorced, instead she would say, "My husband graduated... I'm single again." She literally couldn't get the word "divorced" to come out of her mouth. I remember how hard it was to say to others, "My father was an alcoholic, and that is how he died." I used to think to myself, "What will others think of him? What will they think of me?" I have met people who can never admit to being wrong. Imagine being in a close relationship or marriage with someone like that. I have often said to couples in conflict, "If you have to be right, you are wrong. If you win an argument, you lose." I say this because that is not what marriage is about—being right and winning. It is about a relationship where we directly experience our human failures and choose to continue to love.

Religion too is not essentially about being right, and a faith community is not essentially about being the people who are "right." Faith, church, and relationships are all about imperfect people who are free to be human, free to admit their failures because that is what it means to be human. And that is precisely where we meet God.

The Navajo Indians were known to make rugs that were considered perfect. But the makers would purposely sew a flaw into the fabric to remind them that we all are imperfect, that only God is perfect. They never wanted to forget that truth and how freeing that can be. Here is an invitation to look at our humanity in a new way. Greatness and success at being human is not the elimination of imperfection, but the ability to incorporate it into our life. To embrace our imperfections and even our failures, to live with them and learn from what they teach us. In my life, embracing imperfection and failure meant accepting the reality of my father's alcoholism and working through its impact on my life. And that has been one of the greatest sources of growth and insight for me.

There is a story about the Renaissance artist Michelangelo and an exquisitely beautiful and marvelous piece of marble, but there was a flaw that ran through it. It was so pervasive that none of the other artists of the time would work with the marble. Michelangelo, however, accepted the marble and used the flaw, wove it into his vision, and eventually created his famous "David," which many scholars consider his greatest work. In fact, the sculpture may arguably be even more spectacular because of the flaw itself.

How wonderful it is to see our flaws and even our failures as having the potential to be our greatest assets, our finest gifts to the people we are becoming.

One of the great gatherings of failure in our modern day is Alcoholics Anonymous. It is so effective that it has become the model for many other anti-addiction programs around the world. The program is centered around twelve "steps," the first two of which are essential:

*Step one: Admit that one is powerless over his/her addiction. In other words, admitting failure.*

*Step two: Acknowledge that there is a higher power, greater than oneself, who can restore one to health and wholeness.*

Indeed, we cannot come to know God except by first coming to know the truth about ourselves, the real truth. Not the "truth" we tell others at parties or in social circles. Not the "truth" we masquerade in at church on Sundays. The real truth—the truth only we know, the truth only God knows. We will never find freedom pretending that we are someone we are not. We cannot know God until we know and accept our entire humanity, in all its goodness and all its destructive tendencies. We cannot experience the resurrection without first going to the cross of failure.

I was working with a married couple that was in trouble. After several weeks, the wife reported during one of our sessions that she had just discovered her husband was having an affair. The intense pain this created in her was heartbreaking to witness. A few weeks later I was alone with the husband. He was not a particularly religious man, so I was taken aback by his question. Out of the blue he stopped our conversation and asked, "Is God with me when I sin?" I was never asked this question before and surprised myself with my spontaneous reply.

"Yes, God is with you when you sin. You may not be with God, but God is with you."

Jesus on the cross makes it possible to say that. The earliest understanding of what Jesus did on the cross was that he took our sins to himself. Therefore we don't come to God by getting rid of our sin or our failure, whatever form it may take. Rather, we come to God in the midst of our sin.

One day, Jesus came across a man named Matthew who was sitting at his customs post, collecting taxes. At the time, this was seen as a despicable act. Tax collectors were viewed by the Jews as unclean and traitorous. They were hated, despised, and shunned by all. (Tax collectors were fellow Jews who collaborated with the Roman oppressors and who normally used their position to make themselves rich at the expense of their own people.) This one day, Jesus stopped and looked at Matthew, and he called him to come and follow him. What is so startling is that Matthew was in the very act of collecting taxes when Jesus came to him and called Matthew to himself. There was no requirement of a prior change in Matthew to "clean up his act," so to speak, before he was called or allowed to come into the company of Jesus. Instead, the invitation was there to come *just as he was*, and the only requirement was Matthew's "yes."

Jesus is clearly comfortable with our humanity and our failures, but are we? The only issue is how we respond to our failure and to the One who is with us in our failure. Two of Jesus' closest followers, who walked with him through his life and in whom Jesus put his trust and hope, were Peter and Judas. Both denied Jesus, but how they dealt with their failure toward Christ is what is most significant. Both men failed to love Jesus, and their failure toward him was great indeed. In response, Judas hung himself. But Peter, at the first chance he got, ran to Jesus when he saw him again in his resurrected form.

What do we do with our failure? Hang ourselves with it, or run with it to the one who loves us and calls us just as we are, failure and all? At the last supper, the night before Jesus died, he left his followers his "Body" and his "Blood." Why didn't he leave his "Aroma" or his "Idea?" Because it is in this body, this blood, this humanity, with all its failure, that God in Jesus came and took us to himself, becoming one with us. It is in this Body and Blood that we have the potential to meet this Jesus. In fact, it is the *only* place we can meet Jesus, and the God he came to reveal.

We have all experienced failure and deep struggle, in whatever form it takes. Many of us may be experiencing this right now. This is our common human experience, and this is the very humanity that God in Jesus took to himself when He became one of us. It is this very human experience of failure that God in Jesus shared with us as He hung on the cross. If this says anything, it says we are not alone and the one who has joined in our failure is the only one who can transform it. This is very good news.

. . .

## PERSONAL REFLECTION

*How do you respond to your failures? Consider that this can be the very source of prayer and openness with God.*

# THERE ARE NO GOD-FREE ZONES

*"Who will separate us from the love of Christ?"*

*~Romans 8:35*

I N THE MOST PARADOXICAL OF STATEMENTS, believers in Jesus see his death on the cross as extraordinarily "Good News." This "foolishness" of God in Jesus is spoken most clearly in his last and final act where we discover just how far the reach of the love of God in Jesus really is. It is a reach without limit. This is very difficult for us to understand since as humans we have no experience of a love without limit. All of us are exquisitely aware of our limited ability to love and to be loved. We have no place in our minds to put such an outlandish belief that love can be limitless. Instead, we respond to this love by continually putting restrictions on the love of God in Jesus. We may invite Christ into our lives and profess our belief in him, but in very subtle and real ways, we do not believe. We place limits and boundaries on his love. Honestly looking within reveals some dark places that we keep hidden and ignore as much as we can, places of shame, guilt, and ugly desire. At some deep psychological and spiritual place within us we push the love of God in Jesus away. "Not here. You cannot come here," we say. "Other places are okay, where I look good or when I am acting religious, but not here." We respond like Peter in the boat when he meets Jesus in a new and wonderful way. "Leave me Lord, I am a sinful man." We are accustomed to being "left alone" in the very places we need him most. Believing in Jesus to come into that place is simply too good to be true or just too frightening. But yet he does.

I would like to recall a story that I have never forgotten. It is a true story of a man I had come to know in a church I was attending. Let us call him Joe. I had known Joe to be a very good man, devoted to his faith community, his wife, and his family. He served others and led a life one could easily admire. Joe was a very quiet man and I had never known how he came to this place of faith and service, but I was happy he had. One day we were at a Christmas party and out of nowhere Joe began to talk to me about his life. He was drafted into the Army as a young man and found himself in Vietnam. While there he met a fellow soldier named Tommy and they quickly became the best of friends. He spoke with a surprising warmth of how wonderful a man Tommy was, his kindness, and extraordinary compassion. Prior to joining the Army, Tommy had been in the seminary to become a priest but had become uncertain and left, only to be drafted. During his time in Vietnam, Tommy became convinced of his calling to the priesthood. Joe spoke with such confidence about how he was sure Tommy would have been the best priest. It was clear how close they had become and how deep Joe's affection was for Tommy. Suddenly Joe became serious and recounted to me a fateful day. There had been a battle and Joe was wounded. Tommy ran to his aid, hoping to pick up his close friend and carry him to safety. On the way Tommy was injured himself and fell to the ground, mortally wounded. Joe crawled over to him and Tommy died in his arms.

Joe went on, "At that moment I was filled with anger and it never left me," he said. "Anger at God, anger at life." He recounted how after he returned from Vietnam he would go to a bar each week to start a fight. Looking for the slightest instigation, he would find someone to hit. Joe was a big man, and I knew I would not have wanted to fight him. Time went on and the anger and the fighting did not cease. One day, as was his usual practice, Joe was at a bar and he slugged someone. The man got up, pulled out a .45 handgun, and shot Joe. The police arrived and took Joe to the hospital and then to jail. As he sat in his cell with a bandage around his side and two broken ribs, filled with anger, something happened. It was Joe's moment. The thought came across his mind, *Tommy did not die for this.* At the same moment he realized as well that Jesus did not die for this either. From that moment on, Joe's life was never the same. His path took him to a new place where I was happily able to get to know him. What struck me so much about Joe's story was not just the beauty of his realization and conversion, but where it happened. It happened in a jail cell, with a bandage around his side, with two broken ribs and a heart filled with anger. It was precisely there that the love of God in Jesus came, for there are no God-Free Zones. There is no place that the love of Jesus Christ cannot and does not reach. That is the extraordinary Good News of Jesus crucified. He never stopped loving and that continues to this very moment with each one of us.

If you find yourself at a dark place in your life right now where you feel alone, afraid, and confused, you are not alone. These are the very places where the love of Jesus appears most clearly and tenderly. All of the bad news in our lives can be the very place for extraordinary good news. Our cross is his and his cross is ours for the love that knows no limit and no boundaries.

· · ·

## PERSONAL REFLECTION

*Is there a place within where you refuse to let love enter and refuse to believe God could love you? If so, consider whether that is the very place where God does. How might that transform your feelings?*

# THE SUFFERING GOD

*"He showed them his hands and his side."*
*~John 20:20*

C HRISTIANITY DOES NOT GIVE US THE ANSWERS to all the questions about human suffering. I do not think that Jesus himself gives us all the answers, but Jesus does give us something: himself. He gives us his presence, in the midst of our suffering, because he shares our suffering. We see this when we look at the cross: Jesus on the cross is the suffering of God. God in Jesus does not take away all human suffering, but shares in it—and that can make all the difference. It can even transform our suffering from despair to hope, from confusion to a new understanding, from alienation to union.

There were a few times during my life when this became real to me. My daughter was five years old when she developed these strange, reddish bruises on her skin during a common viral illness. The doctor looked at them and put her in the hospital. They ran an IV and he examined her more thoroughly. I will never forget him taking me out in the hallway and saying, "Dad, this doesn't look good." I thought someone had punched me in the stomach. He described how she had an adverse reaction to the virus, and she was bleeding internally. She was rushed to Children's Hospital of Philadelphia, the next forty-eight hours would tell the tale one way or another.

I remember sitting in the hospital room with my wife, who was then eight months pregnant, as my daughter was lying in a bed, all hooked up to IV's and machines. It was nighttime and it felt dark. Yet somehow in the midst of the shadows, I sensed and knew we were not alone in this pain and anguish. I knew there was Another, and this gave me peace and hope. After a week my daughter left the hospital. Through it all, I knew I was not alone, and that knowledge made all the difference.

Another time I had a similar experience was when my mother came to visit us after the birth of one of our children. My father had died when I was young, so my mother and I were very close. This woman who had never been sick a day in her life suddenly came down with a severe headache and could not even stand up. After visiting the doctor she was put in the hospital, and we watched as she slipped into a coma before our eyes. She had bacterial meningitis and remained in a deep coma for six weeks. I will never forget the doctor talking to my family in the hallway of the hospital, telling us to "pray that she dies, there are worse things than death." In his view, if she lived, which seemed unlikely, she would be so damaged that life would not be worth living. We prayed anyway that she would live.

Days turned into weeks and weeks into months. For eleven months she remained in the hospital with our family by her side. Three times during this period the doctors called our family, believing that they were "losing her." It was the most emotionally painful and exhausting time of my life. All the while we were sustained by one thing: We were not alone. Faith is the assurance of things unseen. Faith is about relationship, it is about presence, a presence that perhaps is given even more when we are most in need and in pain.

Finally, after nearly a year spent in the hospital, we were able to bring her home. She lived another twenty years and during that time, she was a transformed person, more alive and free than I had ever known her.

Each of these events has shown me how the very experience of human suffering can be transformed by the reality of faith in God, who suffers as well. To meditate on the God who suffers on a cross leaves only one conclusion: that God has entered our suffering and shares it with us, even now.

I have met and read about marvelous people of faith who have suffered much more than I could ever imagine and whose response to that suffering, because of their faith, is remarkable.

Elie Wiesel, who suffered in a concentration camp and lost his family before his eyes said, "Because I hope, I know there is a God." Corrie ten Boom, who likewise suffered in a concentration camp and watched her sister die, said, "No pit is so deep that God is not yet deeper." Jesuit priest Fr. Jon Sobrino happened to be away from his home in El Salvador when armed men entered and killed six of his fellow Jesuit priests, as well as their housekeeper and her daughter. At his first public address after this tragedy, he spoke about "Christian Joy."

Where does all this come from? A Jew, a Protestant, and a Catholic. They don't think the same, and they have different theologies. At the same time they share something of the mystery that is the Crucified God, the Suffering God, who has entered into our suffering.

Bernie Mac, the late comedian and actor, wrote in his autobiography *Maybe You Never Cry Again* about the reason why he became a comedian. He was raised in poor circumstances in Chicago by a single mom. He writes:

> *One night, I come in and find my mama in front of the TV, cryin'. And you know how it is when you're a little kid: Your mama cryin', you gonna be cryin' in a minute. "What's wrong, Mamma?" I ask her. "Nothing, baby... Sometimes I think sad thoughts." "What thoughts?" She didn't answer. She was lookin' at the*

*TV. Black guy's talkin' to Ed Sullivan. I look at him,*
*but I don't hear but a few words. And I can't make*
*them out anyway, see, because suddenly my mama's*
*laughin' to bust a gut. Her whole lap's shaken'. I got*
*to hold on tight or get thrown clear across the room.*
*I turn to look at her—this is the same woman that*
*was cryin' a second ago?—then I turn back to the*
*TV. "Who that man, Mama?" She's still laughin'. Takes*
*her a while to catch her breath. "Bill Cosby, son. He's*
*a comedian." A comedian? "What's that?" I look*
*over at this Bill Cosby. I don't know what he's talkin*
*about—but I know that whatever it is, it's got power.*
*"That's what I want to be, Mama. A comedian. Make*
*you laugh like that, maybe you never cry again."*

Bernie Mac became a comedian to get the power that would take away his mother's tears. The direction of his life was set because of those tears, because of his love for his mother. It must be the same with the God of Love who looked upon us and saw the tears of our humanity, the tears of all humanity throughout all of time, and was so moved that he could not take it anymore.

The God of Love is wrecked by our tears. It was this that moved God to send Jesus Christ into our midst. This Jesus, the tears of God. God became one of us, lived with us, and died for us, and perhaps it is in this great act that the power is found to wipe away our tears. Now we will never cry alone, and one day we will never cry again.

. . .

## PERSONAL REFLECTION

*Can you think of a time of suffering in your life when you felt particularly close to God or especially open to God? How does it feel to think that God is moved by our tears and our suffering and that God suffers with us?*

# HOPE

*"Hope does not disappoint."*
~*Romans 5:5*

A T OR NEAR THE TOP OF MOST MOVIE CRITICS' lists for the greatest movie of all time is *Citizen Cain*. The movie begins with the main character's death and his final word, "Rosebud." From that point on, the movie is all about trying to figure out what that word meant. Why? Because we all know that someone's last words are given a special meaning and significance. A person's last words often tell you something about the essence of who they were and what their life was really all about. The same can be said of Jesus, whose last words were: "My God, my God, why have you forsaken me?" (Mark 15:34) At first glance these words sound pretty depressing, but in fact, Jesus was quoting a well-known psalm of trust, Psalm 22, and all who heard his words knew exactly what he meant—and it must have been startling to hear!

Here was Jesus, hanging on a cross, the most awful form of death in the ancient world, reserved for non-Roman citizens. Here is Jesus, suffering in this way and yet, somehow, still trusting. Jesus' suffering was real and complete, and there was no pass for him even if he was God. Jesus not only suffered the physical torment of the cross, but he also faced the void and emptiness of his approaching death alone with no one to companion him, not even the comfort of his Father. When Jesus on the cross looked up at the sky, he saw only sky, for he was left to die alone.

Can you imagine the level of faith Jesus must have had to *still* trust God from the cross, from the darkest of places such as that? Jesus experienced true abandonment and died in true trust all at the same time. His deep anguish before God was real, yet still he trusted, still he loved, and still he forgave. Jesus never ceased to love during his time on earth and that, more than anything else, is what he gave us. It is not how much Jesus suffered, but how much he loved that saved us.

I have witnessed this hope alive today in followers of Jesus, sometimes in extraordinary ways. One of my best friends, and one of the most wonderful people I have ever met, is Fred. Fred is one of those truly good people. I have never heard him say an unkind word about anyone. He is a person of deep faith, great love for his wife and children, who is always ready to lend a helping hand to someone in need. Everyone who meets Fred likes him; it is hard not to. Several years ago he was cleaning a water pump and it exploded in his face. As a result, he suffered a severe and traumatic brain injury. While he was in a coma, with the outcome unknown, I would go to the hospital each day and sit in the waiting room with his family and friends. One day I happened to be alone in the hospital waiting room with his wife, Lori, and she asked me to go and visit Fred in his room in the trauma unit with her. We stood by his bed. Fred was hooked up to all kinds of machines, and you could hear their sounds, the hissing and the beeping. You could see the different colored lights and unintelligible numbers and graphs displayed on screens and detect the particular smells which characterize all intensive care hospital rooms.

The room had only a half wall and nurses and doctors were coming in every minute or so to check some monitor or another. I was standing in silence in this room, deep in thought and raw emotion when Lori turned and asked me to pray with her. Naturally I said yes, assuming we would pray quietly, but Lori then said, "Fred likes the psalms, so let's pray nice and loud in case he can hear us in his coma." Lori proceeded to take out two books of the Psalms, one for me and one for her, and we proceeded to pray the psalms, back and forth, out loud, for all to hear as we stood around Fred. Admittedly, I was somewhat uncomfortable, as I am not accustomed to praying out loud in hospitals, especially one so open for all to hear. After we finished, Lori said, "Fred loves to sing hymns," and she asked me once again to join her. She picked out one of Fred's favorite Christian hymns and asked once again that we sing nice and loud so Fred might be able to hear us in his coma. We began to sing, nice and loud. When we finished, we sang another. There we were, praying psalms and singing hymns over Fred's broken body.

I will never forget the faith of this woman who invited me to join her as we stood together in the midst of suffering and potential death. I realized, at that moment, that this is where the God in Jesus stands, and this is what disciples of Christ do. They bring faith to bear in the darkest of places.

I was stretched in my faith that day, and I was inspired by the one who stood with me, who was in much greater anguish than I but nonetheless still trusted in Jesus, whom she somehow knew had not abandoned her, Fred, or their family. This kind of faith is not only challenging. It is also attractive, compelling, and I would say powerful. It enables one to stand with a head held high when everything around is dark and grim.

Pliny, a second century historian, wrote about the early Christians, saying, "They rise before dawn, sing hymns antiphonally, and worship Jesus as God." Christians did this in a world where three-quarters of the population were slaves and the scale of human suffering was far greater than we could imagine today. For the early Christians, to sing hymns of joy to the one who was crucified was an act of great faith, a faith they discovered could endure even in the midst of struggle, confusion, rejection, suffering, and death. It is no different today. We find ourselves in crisis, pain, or confusion, and it is in these most unlikely of places that we are invited to faith. It is in these most unlikely of places that Jesus shows up. When we choose to have faith that looks beyond the circumstances, when we choose to put our trust in the one who shares our human pain and suffering, we discover the power of transforming hope.

. . .

## PERSONAL REFLECTION

*Think of someone of faith and hope who has inspired you. How can you use their life as a model to bring faith and hope into your life?*

# GOING TO JESUS

*"Mary Magdalene and the other Mary were*
*there, sitting opposite the tomb."*
*··Matthew 27:61*

F OR ME, THE MOST POIGNANT SCRIPTURE PASSAGE
in the New Testament is Matthew 27:59-61:

*So Joseph took the body and wrapped it in a clean*
*linen cloth and laid it in his own new tomb, which he*
*had hewn in the rock. He then rolled a great stone to the*
*door of the tomb and went away. Mary Magdalene and*
*the other Mary were there, sitting opposite the tomb.*

Women in the biblical world are "the weaker sex," yet these
two women rallied their strength when they broke the law to go out
alone at night to the tomb where Jesus lay. In total disillusionment
and despair, they still sought out Jesus and waited silently by his
tomb. Here were these two women, going to Jesus, the only Jesus

they knew, the dead Jesus, and sitting in silence before Him.

That is faith.

It only follows then, that Mary Magdalene was the first to meet the risen Jesus.

In gazing upon the cross, in coming to God in the truth and reality of who we are, in recognizing how God has chosen to participate in all that is human through the person of Jesus, we as imperfect creatures actually get the opportunity to meet God Incarnate, to meet a new life, a new hope. In this, even death is overcome.

It was "a great stone" (Matthew 27:60) that they put before the tomb of Jesus. The obstacles to faith are large indeed, and we all know this because we all have them. Often our obstacles seem insurmountable and other people can only help so much in removing them. In the final analysis, it is God alone who removes all that stands in the way of faith. Indeed, when the women arrived at the tomb, "the stone, which was very large, had already been rolled back" (Mark 16:4). Our journey of faith is to go to the tomb, to go to Jesus, with all our doubts, questions, problems, concerns, religious issues, personal agendas, fears, hurts, anger, insecurity, betrayals, and feelings of loneliness—and bring it all to him. Even when Christ seems so very far away from us; even when he seems dead. Our task is not to worry about how to move the stone; rather, our task is just to go to the tomb in faith, because faith is about movement, it is about going to God no matter what. God will remove the very large stones that get in our way. We, in turn, are called to sit in silence, to present ourselves before the crucified Christ, bringing with us all that we are, just as we are.

I was raised with religion, but God was always on the outskirts of my life. With my father not present much in my life, I was "fathered" more and more by my peers and the culture around me, and I began to take on the way of life and thinking of those around me. My friends, rock music, going out, experimenting with drugs, drinking, chasing girls—these were at the center of my life. One day my father suddenly began to bleed internally and was rushed to the hospital, and two days later he was dead. I was sixteen years old. And I was very scared.

Not long after, I talked to a relative who was a priest, and he told me to listen to my father's funeral. I did—for the first time I really listened. The words, the prayers, and the Scripture seemed to jump out at me. I prayed like I had never prayed before.

*Help.*

That was it, "Help," but it was with *my whole being,* from deep within my heart at a very dark time. What happened next is hard to describe, I felt a presence in that church. It was very real and it was with me. I felt a peace and an impression within myself that *I was loved* and that everything was going to be all right. I knew when I left that church that "something" was real or that "someone" was real, and I knew that my family and I would be okay. My life has never been the same.

In a place of death, I found a new life.

Once that new life is discovered, it is transformative. It changes the way we think, act, and how we respond to the events of our life. It was the faith in the lives of the women who went to the tomb that enabled them to go in the first place. Even in the finality of death, there was still a hope and trust within them that made this movement of faith possible. They had come to know something of this Jesus in their life with him that gave them the ability to still trust and wait, silently looking in his direction in their darkest hour. Somehow they still trusted that this Jesus was not completely absent from them even though the circumstances certainly said he was. That faith reveals a level of trust that can transform all the struggles, crises, and uncertainties of our lives. It gives us the good news to triumph in bad times. My wife, Helen, tells the story of a woman who embodied that faith and trust.

At the time, Helen was only nineteen years old and her own faith was not a living reality. It was her first day at a new job as a nurse's aide in a major city hospital. Needless to say, she began the day already quite nervous, not knowing what to expect and if she would be up to the task. It was not long before she noticed the staff nurses on the floor talking among themselves about a patient whose doctor had just told her that her condition was terminal. Not even these career nurses wanted to go into the patient's room, so they turned to Helen and told her to go in and check on her. As Helen entered the patient's room she saw a woman in a hospital bed and she heard the soft sounds of weeping coming from the woman's husband and young son who were at her bedside. The woman must have realized the look of terror on Helen's face, as she motioned her to come in. Helen then noticed that the woman was sitting up in bed with a bible open before her. She said to Helen, "It's okay, dear. It's okay. I am ready. I am ready." Helen never forgot those words. Though Helen's faith was not alive at the time, she recognized something in this woman that engaged her like nothing had before: the reality of faith and what it could mean in her life. Helen could feel the genuine depth of what those words represented for this woman. Her countenance was peaceful and assured, even though she had just been told she was going to die. Helen had entered the room feeling it was her job to comfort this patient, but in reality the woman was comforting her. This encounter tugged on Helen's heart and mind and caused her to wonder about the faith this woman possessed, and she began to consider it for herself as well. It is this dimension of faith, the power it gives us to face our own mortality with hope and assurance, that is so compelling for those who see it and so transforming for those who possess it. This is the faith of the women who went to Jesus' tomb, and this is the faith that is offered to us all.

. . .

## PERSONAL REFLECTION

*Consider the attitude of the woman of faith in Helen's story. How do you think you would have responded in her place?*

# WALKING THE
# ROAD TOGETHER

*"While they were talking and discussing,*
*Jesus himself came near and went with them."*
*~Luke 24:15*

I N LUKE'S GOSPEL, WE FIND THE STORY OF TWO
of Jesus' disciples walking on the road to Emmaus. They walked
with very heavy hearts, conversing and debating. The one
in whom they had put all their hope, Jesus, had been killed on a
cross, and this was most likely the topic of their conversation. Now
that Jesus was gone, they were leaving town in despair. In Greek,
their "conversing" is better translated as a "deep conversation,"
a "very serious talk," a deep, profound sharing of the mind and
heart. The two followers of Jesus shared with one another from
a very deep place, pondering their circumstances in the midst of
personal turmoil. What happened next is most remarkable: Jesus
showed up, walked with them, and joined their conversation.

Like the disciples on the road to Emmaus, many of us are

struggling at this very moment, questioning our circumstances, on the brink of giving up hope. But like the disciples, we must remember that this is precisely when Jesus shows up. When we share deeply with another disciple the questioning and turmoil deep within our hearts and minds, we create a place where Jesus can come. Our confusion and pain can provide an opportunity to create a "space" for God to enter and be at work in our lives.

It is clear from this story that discipleship is not about superficiality. It is not simply talking about the weather and sports. Our gathering together as a church is not just about attending events that we think religious people are supposed to attend. No, it is about the profound sharing of life and faith with other disciples, the sharing of both the light and the darkness we experience on the journey of faith—especially the darkness, since that is where Jesus shows up. So if we have lost our jobs or our money, if we are feeling distant from God and asking big questions like "why me," then we stand in a space filled with the potential to meet the risen Jesus. It only requires that we open it up to another who is on the journey of faith with us. This is the great gift of church, of community on the road of faith. If there is one place where we can share deeply it must be in this community of disciples.

John Henry Newman used the phrase, "heart speaks to heart" as a motto for his life. He knew and believed that, "So much holiness is lost to the church because brothers and sisters refuse to share the contents of their hearts one with another." So much holiness is lost to the church and to our own lives because we play silly little social games with one another instead of opening up the contents of our hearts to one another. If we want spiritual meaning and freedom, if we want to know the presence of the Risen One, then we need to open up. We all need to find another in whom we trust and can walk the journey of faith together, especially in the darkest times that we all experience in life. In the gospel retelling of the encounter on the road to Emmaus, we also find Jesus interpreting Scripture to the disciples and finally being recognized in the breaking and blessing of the bread. All of this extraordinary revelation would never have happened without the conversation along the way that set the stage. This earliest of places where the risen Jesus is encountered in the breaking of the bread began in the conversation before the meal ever took place. It all begins in the sharing of one disciple with another. The conversation creates the place for Jesus to enter and from there so much more can happen and be revealed. This is why we have church.

I would like to share a story about the kind of power that is present when people come together in openness and sharing of the human heart with one another.

In the city of Philadelphia there is a local radio program called "Voices of the Family," and the director of the program is a psychologist named Dan Gottlieb. It is a good program, and I listen to it when I can. I had known that Dan was a paraplegic, but I never knew how until one day on the program he told his story. Years before

Dan had been in a very serious car accident and ended up in the hospital. Early one day, he received the news that he would never walk again and would be confined to a wheelchair the rest of his life. That evening he was lying in darkness in deep despair. He wanted to die. The nurse on the evening shift came up to him and said, "You're a psychologist. Doesn't everyone consider suicide once in their life?" He replied, "Let's talk." After her shift the nurse came to his bedside and they talked for some time. As it turned out, the nurse herself was considering suicide. Through the conversation, Dan was able to help her see the value of life. In reality, though, the conversation may have helped him even more.

Dan said, "She saved my life. She shared her pain with me and asked something from me." This was quite a scene. Two people, talking in the darkness, both contemplating suicide, sharing their pain and profound struggle and finding life and hope. That is a sign of the redemptive work of God, when two people share the contents of their hearts one with another it creates a holy opening to God. If we turn our emptiness, struggle, and confusion over to God in the process of sharing it with another, we find the freedom to let God be God, to let God work through us and through the other person. We don't discover that all our questions are answered or that all our problems are solved, but we do find a previously unrecognized transforming presence that is made known to us in the conversation along the way. Discovering spiritual meaning in our lives, encountering the presence of God, is not so obtuse, mystical, and foreign. It can be as close as another person. The genuine sharing of the truth of our life with another can be the very place where all this begins to happen. The isolation of ourselves from others is the very place where it does not. Especially during times of crisis and uncertainty, it makes so much sense not to attempt to travel this road alone but to share our struggles with another person. Being open to this kind of dialogue with another and looking for those with whom this could possibly take place is an important spiritual discipline, one that is available and accessible to us all.

. . .

## PERSONAL REFLECTION

*What is deep within my own heart and mind right now?*

# THE END IS THE BEGINNING

*"With that their eyes were opened and they recognized him."*
*~Luke 24:31*

ONCE, TWINS WERE CONCEIVED. WEEKS PASSED and they developed. As they grew, they sang for joy.

"Isn't it great to be alive!"

Together the twins explored the womb. They found their mother's life cord, they shouted for joy.

"How great is our mother's love that she shares her very life with us!"

As weeks passed, the twins began to change.

"What does this mean?" said the one.

"It means that our life in the womb is coming to an end," said the second.

"But I don't want to leave the womb! I want to stay here forever!" said the first.

"We have no choice," said the second. "Besides, maybe there is life after birth."

"How can that be?" said the first. "We will shed our mother's cord, and how is life possible without it? Besides, there is evidence that there were others in the womb before us, and none of them has ever come back to tell us there is life after birth. No, this is the end!"

And so the first twin fell into despair, saying, "If life in the womb ends in death, what is its purpose? It's meaningless! Maybe we don't even have a mother. Maybe we made her up."

"But we must have a mother!" said the second. "How else did we get here? How else do we stay alive?"

And so the last days in the womb were filled with deep questioning and fear.

Finally, the moment of birth arrived. When the twins opened their eyes, they cried for joy.

•   •   •

In the end, there is a change that will come to each and every one of us. It may be difficult or not, but one thing is for certain: It will be unlike any other change we have ever known or imagined. This is one change, no matter how much we prepare, that will still be unexpected. The final puzzle we put together, or the one that is put together for us, will be the one we face when we die.

This is the greatest mystery of our lives, and the Christian belief surrounding death is one even more outlandish than the birth of God among us, more wonderful than the stars in the sky and the universe we live within. At the same time, it is the one singular belief that ultimately has the most importance for our lives, the one most affected by the quality of our listening, looking, effort, and humility in this life. We all die—the statistics on death are still around 100%. Even Jesus died. The good news is not that we die, but that our lives do not end with death, even though everything about death seems to tell us that they do.

On the purely physical level, this is obviously quite a contradiction. We all know what happens to our bodies once we die. We return as dust to the world from which we came. But there is a future beyond this physical realm, and we will, in some way, still be alive.

There is one ultimate belief about Jesus left for us to examine, one that surpasses everything else said about him and the one on which all other belief in him hinges: that Jesus rose from the dead and is alive here and now. It obviously makes a big difference whether we think someone is dead or alive. For one, we expect a lot more from someone who is alive than from someone who is dead. If someone is alive, he/she can still speak to us, we can encounter him or her every day, continue to grow in relationship and share our lives. The dead, on the other hand, are over with. We have our memories and thoughts of the lasting impression they made on our lives, but nothing new is happening. The impact of the dead on us begins to fade as we move on with our lives.

So whether Jesus is dead or alive is the ultimate question, and there is certainly no middle ground. Someone is either dead or alive. The belief that Jesus rose from the dead and is alive among us is a belief with consequences like no other. This distinguishes the Christian view of Jesus from all other perspectives on him, and what it means is not that Jesus started breathing again after a near-death experience. No, Jesus' resurrection is a totally new life altogether. He takes his body with him, but *transforms* his body and begins a new and more wonderful existence, one that is now even more "alive" and powerful than before.

The gospels report that Jesus came back in order to show and offer this new life to his disciples, that they might encounter him and enter into a new experience of him as alive and live intimately with him. Believers testify that this experience of the risen Jesus has continued ever since, and it continues even today. God is now present with us in a way that is more accessible than would be possible with a human body. What this means for us is that at any time, in any place or human circumstance, one can encounter this risen Jesus. This experience is like a taste, a down payment on what is yet to come after we die. Belief in life with God after death is not just wishful thinking; rather, it is based on the fundamental experience of the risen Jesus in our lives, right now, as a living person in our midst, the reason for the hope in what is to come.

Another way to consider this is by examining the Greek word for "time." There are actually two words that the Greeks used for "time." *Cronos* means time on the clock—the day, hour, and minute. *Kairos* means important time—time filled with meaning and effect in our lives. A Kairos time would be the time you asked someone to marry you, the time your child was born, the moment you found out a loved one passed away—it is an event like no other. The day and hour are irrelevant but the time has ultimate meaning and power in our life. These Kairos times are life-changing events and are never forgotten.

"Jesus is risen" means that Jesus now dwells in God's time, Kairos time. It is a time which knows no time and is filled and overflowing with meaning and importance for all time. It is the time of saving grace for all of us. Jesus is present always, and when we encounter him we know it. This is what Jesus is getting at when he says, "blessed are your eyes, for they see, and your ears, for they hear." (Matthew 13:16) When we experience the risen, living Jesus, we finally see. We finally hear. All of our listening and looking, effort and humility, has ultimately brought us to this "blessed" place where we get to see him and hear him and experience his love present with us. This encounter continues to grow throughout our lives, and as our bodies grow older the life of the risen one within us continues to grow as well, pointing to the "more" which is yet to come. It points to the wonder and glory of having life fully with God after death, something that surpasses all other wonder and glory of this life on earth because this is why we were ultimately created in the first place: that we may one day be with God face to face, to see it all, to have it as our own. "What no eye has seen, nor ear heard, nor the human heart conceived, what God has prepared for those who love him." (1 Corinthians 2:9) One day, we will finally "see" it all, and finally "hear" it all. The looking and listening will be over, for we will be given all we have searched for.

So what will happen when we die?

While of course I do not pretend to know what will happen in the afterlife, if any of what I have discussed in this book is true, the one thing of which we can be certain is that love itself is waiting, looking out over the horizon, longing to embrace us. It would be something akin to the ready love described in the parable of the prodigal son. When we die, we will meet this God who is our father who is waiting for us and has been since the beginning of time. God will smile with joy at our sight and begin to run in our direction with his arms outstretched, longing to embrace us. What do we do in this scene? How will we react? Will we hesitate, freeze and become motionless? Will we not react at all because we simply do not know what to do? Perhaps we will turn and walk away or even run in the opposite direction, since this is what we did in our lives whenever this love came our way. Perhaps we will remain where we stand and only wave hello and keep our distance. Maybe we will let God approach and we will put out our hand for a handshake so we can stay in control of what is happening. We may even give God a little pat on the back and smile a bit as we do. How we respond will be determined by how we respond in our lives here and now. If there is separation from God after death it will be for those of us who do not know how to respond to unfailing love and mercy. Let us not be like the twins in the opening story, living only in deep questioning and fear, totally unprepared for the marvelous life that awaits. We are offered to begin this eternal life here and now in receiving that love and mercy that is waiting for us, looking in our direction. If this experience of mercy begins now then our response at our death may be very different.

It is possible that we will respond with explosive joy and run into God's arms. At this moment we will fully know and experience God's warmth and depth of love for us. We will feel the eternal joy of God. Perhaps we may even feel a joyful tear from God's eyes, as well as recognize what has been at stake all along: nothing less than eternal life and the embrace of divine love.

What if the Christian belief is true? What if there is a life after this one? Long before Christianity came on the scene, the Greek philosopher Euripides said, "Perhaps life is death and death is life," meaning that we are dying now but will live after death. It could be that death is not death at all for us who live in God, but instead only a birth to a new life. Substantiated for us not as a philosophical tenant, or wishful thinking, but because a living, risen person is in our midst that we "know" to be true because we have encountered him in our lives here and now. This is the very heart of the Christian story. Augustine put it this way: "We gave to God what He did not have the ability to give to Himself, death. So He could give to us what we did not have the ability to give to ourselves, life." To discover this life, this wonderful good news, would indeed change everything. Our lives would be different, with a new trajectory and understanding because our eyes would be opened and we would recognize the risen Jesus, alive.

• • •

## PERSONAL REFLECTION

*Meditate on and imagine the arms of divine mercy*
*waiting to embrace you. How does this feel?*

# DON'T WAIT

*"The time is fulfilled..."*
*~Mark 1:15*

THE EARLIEST WRITTEN GOSPEL IS MARK. The first words out of Jesus' mouth, as recorded by Mark are these. "The time has come, and the kingdom of God is close at hand. Repent and believe the Good News." (Mark 1:15)

This "time" that Jesus speaks of, the moment that has arrived, the privileged time, is the Kairos time that we have spoken of. In his book *And Now I See*, Robert Barron describes it as "Something that human beings have been longing for and striving after and hoping to see has appeared, and the time is now for a decision, for action. Jesus' very first words are a wake up call, a warning bell in the night, a summons to attention." There is an urgency in the words and passion of Jesus. The time is now. Do not let it pass you by.

Jesus is impatient with only one thing: postponement. That is one option he never offers us. I have seen many people, after they have considered the possibility of faith, respond with a common theme, usually to themselves, "I will get to that later." They say to themselves: "Why now? What is the urgency here? Can we not become believers at any time, so why not wait till later?"

There are two reasons why we should not wait. First, because discovering faith is a process and there is no guarantee we will ever begin. This was driven home for me in a powerful way when a friend of mine, John, and I were discussing this very issue. John told me to tell his story to people who think like that.

As a young man, John was a member of one of the very early Marine contingents sent to Vietnam. John was proud to be a Marine and proud to be fighting for his country. One day on patrol John stepped on a land mine. His leg was blown off just above the knee. What was left looked like spaghetti strands hanging from his leg. Immediately a fellow Marine picked him up and carried him to a helicopter to be evacuated. As they took off, the Vietcong began shooting at the helicopter. A firefight ensued as the machine gunner on the helicopter returned fire while John lay beneath him on the floor in the tight quarters of the chopper. The medic on board began working on John and had torn off his shirt, exposing his bare chest to the red-hot casings from the machine gun as they fell on John's chest, burning him. The scars are still visible today. Eventually they arrived at a MASH unit in the jungle. With all haste he was brought in and laid on an operating table. John still remembers how the edges along the side of the operating table had what looked like gutters to collect blood.

John was in a serious, life-threatening situation. His loss of blood was great and John knew that imminent death was a very real possibility. Just before John was about to lose consciousness from the loss of blood he saw a priest walk in the door towards him. John knew he had come to pray with him and to help him prepare to face his likely death. John's last conscious thought was, *What is he doing here? Just bring in the doctor.*

Some may think that a reasonable thought, to want a doctor in the condition he was in. But John told me the story to reveal something else that was present within him—his complete and utter willingness to die without God. John was not a person of faith at this time and he brought who he was to his place of imminent death. Nothing changed. The way he was before this incident was how he was willing to meet his end. John's story made me realize just how very probable it really is for those of us who have lived a certain way and formed our lives and consciousness accordingly to never change.

I will never forget the look on John's face as he, now a man of great faith, recounted this incident from so long ago. Normally a jovial, lighthearted person with an engaging smile, John looked stern and his voice was serious, almost cold. It was clear to me that this memory, not of the physical suffering and trauma, but of the spiritual emptiness, was chilling.

John's story had a startling affect on me. I understood the exigency of Jesus found in the gospels where we find Jesus crying out to us not to wait, not to hold back, not to live in the illusion of self-satisfaction. We should not wait until later because later may never come. Discovering God and understanding our faith is not something that normally happens in an instant and it's not a game that we play. There is no simple formula, like a series of prayers, to guarantee our faith. It is about the opening of the human mind and heart to the unconditional love of God. That does not come easily or lightly to those who are unaccustomed to doing so. Just as we find it difficult to trust another person, we often find it difficult to trust our lives to God. Faith is a process we become fully engaged in and are utterly transformed by; otherwise it is not real.

Of course, God is patient and waits for us, even if it pains God to do so. (Just as it would for anyone who is forced to wait for the one he or she loves.) Yes, God will receive us at any time and in any circumstance, no matter what we have done and where we find ourselves, but if we can begin our journey to understanding faith and God's divine love for us, then we can begin our new life and also begin to build God's kingdom here on earth, now.

The second reason we should not wait is what possible reason can there be for waiting? What is being offered is so much better and it begins now! Why miss out on this for one more day, one more minute, one more second? Many people find their time filled with other distractions: a new job, children, the pursuit of material wealth so that they can provide a safe and comfortable home for their families (all admirable pursuits on their own), but without faith, what is the point?

Let me put it another way. To quote from the movie *When Harry Met Sally,* "when you realize you want to spend the rest of your life with somebody, you want the rest of your life to start as soon as possible." Starting on our spiritual journey is an opportunity to start the rest of our lives with God. It will give us the strength and courage to weather the storms that most assuredly come our way, and it helps us to more fully enjoy the gifts of this life immediately. This sentiment is no better expressed than in the words found in Psalm 84: "For a day in your courts is better than a thousand elsewhere. I would rather be a doorkeeper in the house of my God than live in the tents of wickedness." May we not allow the good of this life to be a substitute for the best.

• • •

## PERSONAL REFLECTION

*In what ways do you find yourself putting God off until later? What might you be missing now?*

# CONCLUSION

RECENTLY I MET WITH A WOMAN TO DISCUSS some of the problems she was facing in her life. After a while she changed the conversation and spoke about the real reason for her visit. She said, "I don't think I believe in God or believe that there is someone out there who really cares for me. I want to have faith. Why do you believe in God?" My initial response was to think to myself, *Well, that is not an easy question to answer.* So I decided I would just be honest. I said, "Because I have met Him." I shared very briefly how I believe I have met God in my life.

So what if you are in the same place as this woman? What if right now you are reading these words and you are thinking to yourself, *I just don't know that I believe there is a God who loves me.* Or what if you are convinced of God's existence, but you wonder about God's presence in your life. Perhaps you just need guidance on how to encounter God. If any of these are the case, then I would like to offer you the same advice I went on to offer that woman:

- *Take twenty minutes every day to sit in silence,* away from noise and distraction, when you are awake and alert and can best focus your mind and heart. Talk to God in your own words. Share the truth of who you are to the one who just might be there listening. Go on to share the contents of your heart in the silence of yourself, in the intimacy of your soul, as an act of seeking one who may be there with you. Then try, if you can, to be completely open and receptive for just one or two more minutes. Do this every day and see what happens.

- *Find some people of faith.* There are no people of perfect faith, but you can and should find a few people in whom you can sense a genuine and living faith. Hang around them and enter into some dialogue from time to time, but most importantly just spend time with them. I believe that faith is "caught" more than it is "taught." When you feel comfortable, consider going to church, where such people gather to pray and express their faith. Pray there, with others of faith and see what happens.

- *Consider reading the Bible.* Read it like it was the first time. Bring the person you are, right now, with all your questions and life experience to the reading. Then listen to what the Scriptures say to you. Do not read the Bible as a history book or as a literal translation set in stone, but as words written for you and to you. Listen to how it might speak to your life, not someone else's.

If you do these things, and you are sincerely open, I am convinced you will begin to discover the presence of divine love, and your life will not be the same. It may happen almost imperceptibly at first, but one day you will recognize something has happened. After this you will be invited to go even further and see that there is more, and more, and more....

We all stand before the mystery of life and the mystery of faith. We are all like my friend Sam on the beach, gazing out over the ocean, asking, *Is it true...is it true...could it be...could it be...?* It is interesting to note that Jesus very rarely asked that we believe in him. What he often said was to trust in him. Jesus spoke of God's love for us being manifested through him, and more than anything else he showed us how to respond: "Do not be afraid." We overcome our fear when we touch a reality that is so much bigger than ourselves and when we discover that reality is pure love for each of us, personally. The miracles of this world point to a reality greater than ourselves. The word translated as "miracle" in the New Testament *(semeion)* literally means "sign." To what are these signs pointing?

The signs are pointing to the possibility of saying "yes" to it all: yes to the mystery of love, yes to the mystery of God, yes to the invitation to faith, yes to the acceptance of mercy.

The icon of Christian faith through all of history was Mary, a woman so obscure and weak in her beginnings. She was young in a world that valued age, female in a world run by males, poor in an age that placed wealth and status above all else. She had no official religious standing, yet it was this woman who was invited to something quite remarkable: to say yes to mystery like no one else and to be a model of that yes for all who would follow. In other words, to trust.

Faith is our yes to that same invitation. That is why Mary is the icon of faith. St. Augustine said, "The greatest event in human history is not the birth of Jesus, but the yes of Mary." Everything depended on Mary's yes. And everything depends on our yes. The poet Angelus Silesius was even more blunt, as he said, "If Christ is born in Bethlehem but not in you, what good is it?" What an extraordinary statement, to imply that the birth of God in Jesus and the death of God in Jesus is virtually useless without our response. Augustine and Silesius are saying that all of it, all the meaning and power it offers us, is lost if there is not a human response to the gift of God in Jesus. It is still the same today.

Augustine put it this way: "May the event you admire in Mary's flesh happen in the intimacy of your soul." But could this actually happen within you? Yes, it could; in fact it longs to happen within you. The event of God in Mary is an event in God's time, in Kairos, and therefore it is timeless. That event is now and can happen in us as well. It is as if God in Jesus is still knocking, not on the doors of homes but on the door of the human heart, still seeking for a place to be born. What will we say? How will we respond?

• • •

Our life is ultimately incredibly short, a nanosecond of time in the universe, and our response is so vitally important. It is a response we alone can make.

Why wait and risk another moment of life? Love is just standing there, looking over the horizon in our direction, waiting for you and for me.

Why not now? Why not say yes? Why not pray the one word that will give to us the one who is himself the living Good News?

# SMALL GROUP DISCUSSION QUESTIONS

. . .
## PART I
. . .

### LISTENING

*It can be very difficult for us to admit when we are wrong, but it is also a necessary step on our path to spiritual growth. It can be even harder to do this when we must admit that a long-held belief may not be as correct as we once thought. Can you think of a time when you had to change your opinion on something that you held dear? What was it, and how did your newfound perspective affect your life?*

## WE ARE WORTH MORE

*Think of the times in your life when you have settled*
*for "well enough." What were some of those? Do you*
*regret your decisions in the past? Is there anything in*
*which you are settling now and feel the need to change?*

## CHANGE

*How do you feel about change? Is it exciting*
*and hopeful, or something you would like to*
*avoid? What is change saying to you?*

## CRISIS

*Where have you experienced the most growth, learning,*
*and personal development in your life? Was it mostly*
*from your successes, awards, and achievements,*
*or from your failures, sufferings, and losses?*

## WHAT MATTERS?

*Ask yourself: Have I ever thought about what is most*
*important to me and what others have told me is most*
*important? Do I see a difference? How well am I living?*

## DECISIONS

*How do you feel about the idea that faith is a daily choice in how you choose to love or not love in each situation of your life, no matter how small?*

## GOOD NEWS, BAD NEWS... WHO KNOWS?

*How does the story by Anthony DeMello speak to your life experience? Have you ever perceived some new occurrence to be bad news, only to see it turn into good news?*

## WHY AM I HERE?

*Have you decided if you view your life as cosmic chance or divine intention? If yes, what helped you make that decision? If not, start this conversation with yourself. It may not be a short one.*

. . .
# PART II
. . .

## HE HAS A NAME. IT IS JESUS.

*"I am a Christian so I can be a human." What does that statement say to you?*

## UNFAILING LOVE

*Love as a concept has been devalued in our society, but the truth that "God is love" has the power to change lives when it is truly realized. In what ways can you live out this truth in your life?*

## FALLING IN LOVE WITH GOD

*How have you allowed yourself to be distracted from the love and wonder that surround you? Did you have a feeling of dullness or emptiness at those times? Have you ever fallen in love with God? Would you like to?*

# THE CHURCH OF THE SECOND CHANCE

*Can you think of a time when you said "no" to God, only to be given a second chance? What happened and how did you react to your second chance?*

# MERCY

*At some point in our lives, we all struggle with Jesus' call to show mercy. Describe a time when this happened to you. How did you behave? How could you have behaved better?*

# THE CRUCIFIED GOD

*What does the phrase, "The Crucified God" and "he was crucified in weakness" mean to you?*

# THE FAILURE OF GOD

*Jesus' disciples viewed his crucifixion as an abject failure, yet from it the early Christians were eventually able to draw strength and ultimate victory. In light of this, how might we see our failures differently?*

## THERE ARE NO GOD-FREE ZONES

*How do you respond to the phrase,*
*"There are no God-Free Zones"?*

## THE SUFFERING GOD

*Have you ever met or read about someone who has*
*suffered much and still has faith, hope, and even joy in*
*their lives? What did you take away from their example?*

## HOPE

*What does it say to us that Jesus died in the midst of*
*true despair and true trust all at the same time?*

## GOING TO JESUS

*Like the women who went to the tomb, are*
*there times in your life when you went to God*
*when God seemed particularly absent? What*
*was it like and what did you learn?*

## WALKING THE ROAD TOGETHER

*Have you ever shared the contents of your heart
with another? If you have, what did you discover?*

## THE END IS THE BEGINNING

*How does the story of the twins speak to you?*

## DON'T WAIT

*What reasons do you have for waiting to know
God? What obstacles stand in your way?
(Remember that these obstacles may be seemingly
good things that make you content to maintain
the status quo and not challenge yourself.)
How can you overcome these obstacles?*

# ACKNOWLEDGMENTS

I AM GRATEFUL TO THE FOLLOWING PEOPLE. Carolyn Aspinal, who encouraged me from the beginning and helped me to stay focused on the goal of this book. Marty Kenny for his support and direction. Meg Monihan, whose excellent editing taught me how to be a better writer. Andrew Yankech, for taking on this project and skillfully improving the text while staying true to its message. It is a gift in life to have people who help you better communicate what you are trying to say.

Finally, to my wife Helen, to whom this book is dedicated. There is much in my life that would not have been without you. This is just one more.

# ABOUT
# THE AUTHOR

J OHN P. LOZANO is a permanent deacon and has worked for 24 years in campus ministry at Villanova University and as an instructor in the department of Theology and Religious Studies. He holds masters degrees in Theology, Counseling, and Liberal Studies. Over the years, John has worked as a marriage counselor, a parish director of adult faith formation, and developed small faith communities, Bible study and retreat programs. He and his wife, Helen, have three children and live outside Philadelphia.

John is the founder of Kairos Missions: a ministry dedicated to helping people from any background better understand, appreciate, and personally engage the Good News of Jesus Christ. He regularly gives retreats, missions, and seminars and can be contacted at www.KairosMissions.org.